# SANE POLITY

Also by William Ophuls

*Ecology and the Politics of Scarcity*

*Requiem for Modern Politics*

*Plato's Revenge: Politics in the Age of Ecology*

*Immoderate Greatness:Why Civilizations Fail*

# SANE POLITY

## A Pattern Language

William Ophuls

Library of Congress Control Number: 2012919004

CreateSpace Independent Publishing Platform

North Charleston, South Carolina

Insanity in individuals is something rare—but in groups, parties, nations, and epochs, it is the rule.

Friedrich Nietzsche[1]

When [Plato and Aristotle] amused themselves writing their *Laws* and their *Politics*, they did it as a game. This was the least philosophic and the least serious part of their life, the most philosophic being living simply and quietly. If they wrote about politics, it was as if to lay down rules for an insane asylum. And if they pretended to talk about it as something important, it was because they knew that the madmen to whom they were talking thought themselves kings and emperors. They entered into their principles in order to make their madness as little harmful as possible.

Blaise Pascal[2]

# Contents

# Preface

Modern political economy, whatever its merits and achievements (which are considerable), is perishing by its own hand. This self-destruction is the direct and logical consequence of following the political principles inherited from Thomas Hobbes and his successors. These principles—along with their associated concepts, beliefs, and practices—are no longer intellectually tenable or practically viable and must be replaced by ones grounded in biological, physical, and psychological reality.[1]

The best way to conceive and shape the political future is not with rigid legal machinery, as is our wont, but instead with flexible design criteria resembling the architectural patterns used for constructing human settlements and dwellings.[2] Here, then, is my proposed pattern language of sane polity—a set of basic principles and practices that, if followed, would render our collective madness "as little harmful as possible."

This is an essay in every sense of the word—a brief trial of one person's ideas intended to stimulate thought and debate, not to be the last word on the subject. Whether I am right or wrong about particular patterns and their implications is not so important. The point is to recognize that the epistemological ground has shifted. We live in a post-mechanical age whose master science will be ecology; political thought and practice must reflect this epochal shift.[3] What follows suggests how we might begin to reconstitute politics in the light of ecology.

# Introduction

Constitutions are an ancient idea. Polities need a foundation, and when they become too large or complex to be governed tacitly—that is, by custom—they require explicit laws. Early legal codes, such as the code of Hammurabi, were quite simple and primarily concerned with crime and punishment. In time, however, the codes evolved into genuine constitutions: a set of basic laws establishing political institutions.

This process reached its apotheosis in the modern age. Inspired by the mechanical worldview, Thomas Hobbes declared the age of natural polity over. Henceforth, political community would be artificially created: "By art is created that **great** LEVIATHAN called a COMMONWEALTH."[1]

The founders of the American polity were the supreme exemplars of this new mode of political thought. Even more mechanically minded than Hobbes, James Madison and his fellow federalists set about constructing a political machine that would foster liberty and forestall tyranny by checking and balancing one aspect of polity with another. The result was, said Benjamin Franklin, "A republic, if you can keep it."[2]

We could not. In 1829, a mere four decades after the Constitution was ratified, a drunken mob laid waste to the White House on the night of Andrew Jackson's inauguration, an episode that symbolically marks the change from republic to democracy. As described by Alexis de Tocqueville, American democracy still retained many republican features, but the ethos of Walt Whitman's "barbaric yawp" increasingly dominated, so the Constitution no longer meant what the founders intended.

However, this was only the beginning of radical change. A catastrophic civil war, a booming population, growing industrial wealth, increased social complexity, a series of imperial adventures, the entry into World War I, an intoxicating boom succeeded by a devastating bust, World War II and an ensuing cold war, still more imperial adventures, and voilà–an American empire that the founders would consider corrupt and tyrannical, a betrayal of their deepest principles.

This is, of course, to make a long and complex story too short and simple, not to say tendentious. (Nor should we overlook the founders' sins against their own principles.) But the point is that the political machinery established by the founders could not withstand the ravages of time. Circumstances changed, but the machinery was fixed. Jury-rigging the Constitution with amendments and court decisions has not been successful in keeping the American polity true to its original principles.

In a previous work, I argued that the epistemological revolution of the twentieth century has decisively overthrown the mechanical worldview.[3] The natural world is not a clock, and human society is not a machine. Trying to order human affairs using mechanical methods will therefore fail. To succeed, we must learn to think and act systematically about economy, society, and, above all, polity.[4] To that end, instead of focusing on the machinery of government, it will be more fruitful to conceive politics in the light of ecology—in other words, to consider how we might model the governance process on the basic physical and biological principles that govern natural processes.[5]

In practice, this means that we need to comprehend and mimic the organic design strategy of nature. We can do this by focusing on dynamics rather than mechanics and by thinking in terms of processes rather than structures. For nature is not a preconceived structure. Rather, it is created by design criteria— for instance, the laws of thermodynamics or the chemical properties of carbon—that order the natural world into the patterns that constitute the rich panoply of life. Even at the level of the organism, says James Gleick, DNA does not specify the "particular spatial structure" of a tree, only "a repeating process of bifurcation and development" that produces its characteristic yet unique shape.[6]

Before Darwin, men and women believed that the deity had ordained creation. We now know that the natural world is the outcome of a process that has no fixed end but that nevertheless evolves purposefully toward ends inherent in the design criteria. Mammals and dinosaurs are very different creatures, but they fit roughly similar niches in roughly similar ecosystems because the design criteria compel beings and systems to arrange themselves in particular ways.

Unfortunately, says Melvin Konner, human society is not an organism and therefore lacks a "natural" homeostatic set point. The "cells" (individuals) have evolved not to support the "body" (society) but to go their own way.[7] There is, therefore, no escape from the design imperative. The form of the polity must be specified in one way or another.

We cannot, of course, simply copy nature's method, but only adapt its design strategy to our own ends. That is, we cannot impose fixed and implacable laws like the laws of thermodynamics and then abscond, letting the chips fall where they may. We must instead continuously employ "art" to achieve an outcome that meets human needs and yet possesses some of the persistence, stability, adaptability, and resilience of natural systems.

The human art of architecture, to which the political art is often compared, can teach us how to use design criteria to create sane polities. This is exemplified in the work of Christopher Alexander and his colleagues, who have reconstructed architectural theory on organic principles. In brief, they expound a design philosophy that they call "the timeless way of building."[8] This philosophy is expressed concretely in a "pattern language" that guides planners, architects, and builders toward creating settlements and dwellings that are practically viable, aesthetically pleasing, and spiritually satisfying.[9]

Alexander's *Pattern Language* identifies 253 patterns ordering every aspect of the built environment, from regions and neighborhoods to room layouts and ornamental details. One such pattern is *Light on Two Sides of Every Room*, which allows an almost infinite number of rooms to be constructed according to the pattern but guarantees that each will have enough natural light to feel comfortable. Another is *Ceiling Height Variety*, which again permits many different types of rooms but ensures that they will cohere into a structure that is neither monotonous nor claustrophobic.[10] Still other patterns enjoin pedestrian-friendly neighborhoods composed of buildings no more than four stories high that are clustered around plazas, markets, and promenades—all with the aim of fostering human scale and social interaction.

What follows is my attempt to devise an analogous pattern language for politics. My aim is not to dictate particular institutions, which must be closely adapted to local conditions. (For instance, combining the institutional framework of representative democracy with the culture of a tribal society is more likely to incite ethnic or sectarian strife than civil compromise.) Rather, I seek to identify the patterns most conducive to polities that are reasonably efficient, humane, harmonious, and ecological—in short, sane instead of mad.

As will be seen, a political pattern language is compatible with the ancient understanding that the best polity is a mixed polity. No one value or dimension of politics, such as liberty or equality, can be exalted over all the others, for each has its characteristic virtues and vices. Thus it is necessary to encourage the former and restrain the latter to create a political ecology that integrates the parts into a harmonious and sustainable whole.

Politics is not so simple, so there are no simple answers. To employ the distinction made famous by Isaiah Berlin, hedgehogs with their one big idea are bound sooner or later to collide with a refractory political reality, whereas the more nuanced, prudent, and sophisticated foxes who know many things are more likely to arrive at workable and lasting solutions to the complex challenges of politics.[11] The patterns that follow are a toolkit for foxes.

# 1

## Nature First

Ecology precedes humanity. Hence nature is the measure of all things. The famous assertion of Protagoras to the contrary is simply wrong on its face: man is an animal who owes his very existence to nature. The human race is the product of eons of evolution and is inescapably intertwined with the natural world—not separate from it, and certainly not above it. Polity, society, economy, and every other aspect of human culture depend totally on the benefits and resources provided by nature. In the end, humanity must tailor the garment of civilization to the measure of ecology.

*Homo sapiens* is a clever, generalist species. Human beings have therefore been able to manipulate the natural world largely to their advantage, especially during the last three centuries. But the castle of human wealth and power rests on an ecological foundation. Humanity must therefore comply with the basic laws of nature that govern the biological world.

To be specific, humankind cannot dump waste products into the environment faster than nature can digest them, use renewable resources faster than nature can replenish them, or consume nonrenewable resources as if they were infinite instead of finite. In other words, humanity cannot both overspend natural income and invade or damage the natural capital that provides the income. Nor can it survive, much less thrive, unless it conforms to natural imperatives and adjusts its social and economic ends to accommodate its ecological means (27. Thermodynamic Economy*).

This does not mean that human beings can live harmlessly. Our very dependence on the complex tissue of relationships that makes up the natural world

---

* The numbered titles between parentheses are cross-references to other chapters that contain related material.

guarantees that we will live at the expense of other creatures. But how we do it matters immensely, says Wendell Berry:

> To live, we must daily break the body and shed the blood of Creation. When we do this knowingly, lovingly, skillfully, reverently, it is a sacrament. When we do it ignorantly, greedily, clumsily, destructively, it is a desecration. In such desecration we condemn ourselves to spiritual and moral loneliness, and others to want.[1]

Exploiting nature without compunction is not necessary for human beings to enjoy a good life (26. Economy of Plenitude). By orienting civilization toward nonmaterial ends—toward making souls instead of consumers—we can become fully human within the bounds set by nature (20. *Paideia*).

# 2

## Community Prior to Individual

Biologically, there is no such thing as an individual. Every organism is a symbiosis of cells that are themselves little symbioses. Organisms also depend for their continued existence on food, air, water, and other natural requisites—that is, on the vast web of interrelationships that constitutes the life process. Each species, each organism is therefore but a little standing wave in the common stream of life, an epiphenomenon that has only a fleeting existence before sinking back into the stream.

In addition, the human species evolved in groups, so *Homo sapiens* is an obligate social animal. Individuals are nothing without the community into which they are born—first the little community of the family that welcomes each infant into the world, and second the larger community of the society that embodies the mores, language, and culture necessary for even the most basic human existence. Nobody bootstraps him- or herself into adulthood or learns a language in isolation.

Politically, except in simple, pre-civilized societies in which the society is also the polity, the individual is inescapably either a subject or a citizen. Government may be relatively formal or informal, big or small, strong or weak. The balance of duties, responsibilities, and rights may also vary according to the society. But in more complex societies, there is always a government charged with defending and maintaining the society's existence—and the interests of the whole have to prevail over the interests of the parts, if only because the existence of the parts depends on the whole. The question is only whether a government will be oppressive and predatory or sane and humane.

By way of summary, John Donne's famous, "No man is an island entire of itself," is more than a metaphysical principle; it is a brute fact of human existence. Yet individual desires and proclivities inevitably conflict with collective needs and values, so the little island of ego tends constantly to diverge from the mainland of polity. How to make the common good prevail over private interest is, therefore, the eternal problem of politics. While there can be no ideal or final solution, there are ways to make the necessary rigor of governance compatible with human dignity and personal rights.

First, most important, if mores are strong, then government can be weak (3. Mores the Keystone). If mores are weak, however, then government will be ineluctably drawn into the ensuing moral vacuum. Thus one of the most critical functions of mores is to inculcate moderation in the citizenry so that they are made aware of the limits to their freedom and of their obligations to the polity (12. Restrained Liberty).

Second, if government is strong where it needs to be strong, then it can be limited in its impact on citizens' lives (7. Strong Governance and 8. Limited Government). That is, there will be few laws and little administration (9. Minimal Laws and 10. Small Administration). In addition, governmental power can be exercised in ways that minimize the corrupting effect of political power (11. Collective Leadership and 16. Wisdom Council).

Finally, if the ethos of the society reflects an exalted ideal, then individuality and polity can peacefully coexist, allowing individuals to flourish along with the society instead of in conflict with it (4. Guiding Ideal and 20. *Paideia*). And if economy is dedicated to plenitude instead of acquisition, then all can enjoy a modest prosperity (26. Economy of Plenitude).

That individual wants must yield to collective needs is unavoidable. It is the price we humans pay for being innately social. But we can structure the polity so that it supports, rather than frustrates, the natural human urge for self-expression and self-fulfillment. A polity dedicated to making souls as well as citizens will enhance freedom even as it limits it.

# 3

## Mores the Keystone

Making polity sane is not easy when the raw material is seriously defective. Men and women may not be devils incarnate, but they are certainly not angels either. Rather, they are born as passionate beings and require intensive schooling to make them fit for society. Children do not need to be taught to be selfish, greedy, contrary, devious, angry, stubborn, envious, untruthful, or disobedient; instead, parents everywhere struggle to rid their children of these and other undesirable traits.[1]

To approach the problem from the other end, society is constituted by its mores—that is, by its customs, usages, and values, particularly those related to morality and good behavior. Thus the idea of a value-free or antinomian society is a contradiction in terms. Unless the population by and large conforms to established moral norms, a society will simply fly apart (4. Guiding Ideal).

In the end, mores determine the character of the polity. Edmund Burke explains why:

> Men are qualified for civil liberty in exact proportion to their disposition to put moral chains upon their own appetites… Society cannot exist unless a controlling power upon will and appetite be placed somewhere, and the less of it there is within, the more there must be without. It is ordained in the eternal constitution of things, that men of intemperate minds cannot be free. Their passions forge their fetters.[2]

A polity in which mores are strong and effective, so that people are on the whole law-abiding, can be governed with a light hand. Citizens will therefore enjoy considerable freedom within the limits set by the laws (12. Restrained Liberty). But when mores are weak and ineffective, people will lack the inner disposition to govern their own will and appetite, so the polity will require both more laws and more aggressive law enforcement. Even so, such an amoral police state is bound for eventual collapse, because when mores are routinely flouted, no amount of policing can stop a downward spiral of corruption.

The ideal, said Hippolyte Taine, is "a state of affairs in which every man is his own constable, until at last none other is required."[3] This ideal is approached only in small bands of hunter-gathers, where bad behavior is easily discovered and swiftly punished. In larger and more complex societies with greater access to privacy, the temptation to bend or break the rules is ever present. Sustaining the moral basis of society is, therefore, by far the most critical task of good governance.

Among other things, government must make the health and welfare of families and, above all, children its highest priority. This is not solely because children are the bearers of the common future (15. Long Time Horizon). It is because mores are necessarily inculcated by the little polity of the family. If the family fails in this regard, then society loses its main defense against demoralization.

Laws, said Jean-Jacques Rousseau, are only the ribs of the arch of polity, whereas mores are the "unshakeable keystone" that holds the arch fast.[4] Mores keep us from yielding to the constant temptation to deviate, wangle, and finagle. If too many yield to this temptation, society unravels, creating a vacuum that will be filled by the magnified and possibly malign power of the state. The equation between morality and polity is ironclad: strong mores foster the benefits of limited government; weak mores entail the evils of unlimited government. Therefore let mores be strong—yet not so rigid that they leave no room for our all-too-human nature (6. Tolerance).

# 4

# Guiding Ideal

No polity can be "a mere alliance" of self-interested individuals, said Aristotle.[1] What makes a political community cohere is "a rule of life"—that is, a shared ethos.[2] Without the social glue provided by an ideal or ideology held in common, a government would have no legitimate authority, and the polity would soon self-destruct in a war of all against all. A people lacking an ideal, said Gustave Le Bon, is just a crowd, and crowds "are only powerful for destruction."[3]

The nature of the ideal is not so important. Cult and religion have usually served as the primary source of the political charisma that confers legitimacy, but these can manifest in various ways—from extremely pious and dogmatic to relatively secular and tolerant. Thus monotheistic Islam, polytheistic Hinduism, animistic Shinto, and nontheistic Confucianism have all been the basis of political order. In the end, what matters is not the source of charisma, only that the polity be seen to enjoy "the mandate of heaven."[4]

Cult and religion normally combine with other ideals and beliefs to lend a unique flavor to a particular civilization or polity. In ancient Greece, a crude piety allied to a rich mythology existed alongside the ideals of *arete* and *paideia*. In traditional Japan, Shinto was the basis of the cult of the emperor, but not to the exclusion of *bushido*, Buddhism, and worship of the aesthetic. In Europe during medieval times, church and state became political allies, with the former upholding the divine right of kings and the latter enforcing the pope's religious monopoly.

In modern times, ideology—that is, secular religion—has mostly eclipsed cult as the locus of political charisma. The former Soviet Union was held together by the ideals and doctrines of Marxist-Leninism, and it collapsed when they no longer inspired allegiance or belief. The United States is held together by a written Constitution that has been largely overtaken by events and by democratic values that seem to be increasingly nugatory, so it may one day meet a similar fate.

Unfortunately, a merely secular polity is almost a contradiction in terms. According to Will and Ariel Durant, one of the most important lessons of history is that "the masses of mankind desire a religion rich in miracle, mystery, and myth."[5] In fact, they continue, "There is no significant example in history, before our time, of a society successfully maintaining moral life without the aid of religion."[6] The mandate must indeed come from "heaven," or it will not be effective.

To put it another way, polity depends ultimately on myth, metaphor, and the like, not the rational mind.[7] But this creates a quandary. Most of the patterns of a sane and humane political system can be created by human effort and ingenuity—that is, rationally—except the most important one of all, namely the polity's core ideal.

That being said, acknowledging that humanity is deeply connected to all of life would be a giant step toward creating a guiding ideal that did not depend on supernatural explanations (1. Nature First). Similarly, a society that offered its members many pathways to individual excellence and lives of many dimensions instead of one would have less need to bolster the authority of the state with supernatural sanctions (20. *Paideia* and 22. Education for Excellence). Indeed, the simple understanding that polity needs to be rooted in the infinite would make room for the mandate of heaven to emerge organically.

# 5

## Prudence

Prudence is applied wisdom: the exercise of sound judgment in practical matters to find the best course of action in a complex and unforgiving world. It is, therefore, the prime political virtue, because failure to find this best course can lead to ruin. Prudence has many aspects (and a long history of discussion within the Western political tradition), but its essence can be captured under three rubrics: realism, calculation, and foresight.

First, a polity must be utterly realistic about human nature. As noted, men and women are a volatile and passionate mixture of devil and angel. (Which tendency dominates depends on governance, public spirit, and mores—see 2. Community Prior to Individual, 3. Mores the Keystone, and 7. Strong Governance.) Theories of government predicated on some other, better class of human being are therefore delusory and dangerous—dangerous because when refractory individuals persist in their old ways, rulers seized by some ideal of social perfection are tempted to force them to adopt new ways whether they like it or not. It is not only more realistic, but also easier and less bloody, to take human nature as it is and to make laws and policies accordingly.

In addition, prudence means being realistic about the limits of human knowledge. We do not know enough to boss the world around. We must, therefore, meet circumstances with an open mind and a willingness to be led by the facts rather than trying to impose our views and aspirations on reality. "The circumstances," said Edmund Burke, "are what render every civil and political scheme beneficial or noxious to mankind."[1]

Second, a polity must calibrate ends to means, never biting off more than it can chew. The need for a careful calculation of probabilities and risks is most compelling in the area of war and peace. Many societies have brought disaster upon themselves by rejecting opportunities for peace out of pride and stubbornness or by starting fights they could not reasonably expect to finish, with Napoleon's invasion of Russia being a classic case in point. Similarly, polities have perished domestically by making social or military commitments exceeding their financial means, which then forces them to adopt bad fiscal and tax policies (28. Pay As You Go and 29. Sound Money). In the end, prudence enjoins modest ends backed by ample means combined with a resolute avoidance of unnecessary risks.

Third, implicit in the above is foresight (15. Long Time Horizon). A polity that does not invest in posterity is not likely to have a brilliant future. If the society consumes instead of saves, or coddles grandparents instead of educating grandchildren, it is going downhill. In addition, if policies are conceived without carefully thinking through the likely first- and second-order (or even third-order) consequences, the almost certain result will be unexpected and often harmful side effects that might have been avoided with a little more forethought (16. Wisdom Council and 17. Technical Board).

Prudence therefore means playing a long game, foreseeing the future needs of the polity and investing resources accordingly. Above all, it means anticipating and forestalling future dangers as Niccolò Machiavelli urges:

I compare fortune [the unpredictability and uncontrollability of life] to one of those violent rivers which, when they are enraged, flood the plains, tear down trees and buildings, wash soil from one place to deposit it in another. Everyone flees before them, everyone yields to their impetus, there is no possibility of resistance. Yet although such is their nature, it does not follow that when they are flowing quietly one cannot take precautions, constructing dykes and embankments so that when the river is in flood they would keep to one channel or their impetus would be less wild and dangerous.[2]

Unfortunately, the prudence that makes life "less wild and dangerous" by taking sensible precautions beforehand is not innate. To the contrary, human beings have a tragic flaw: hubris. They readily lose touch with reality, overestimate their abilities, and overlook future risks and consequences, especially when intoxicated by power. But to overreach, to go beyond what is practically feasible or humanly possible, invites retribution in exact proportion to the extent of the overreaching. The sole defense against the nemesis that implacably punishes hubris is prudence—steadfast realism, careful calculation, and keen foresight. That prudent governance will result in a less-than-perfect polity inhabited by recalcitrant people who can be preserved from anarchy but not from every form of stupidity, sin, and vice is something that we must simply learn to accept (6. Tolerance).

# 6

# Tolerance

Tolerance is essential to a sane polity. Gross intolerance leads ultimately to pogroms, ethnic cleansing, civil wars, killing fields, and other atrocities. Even in its milder forms—discrimination, backbiting, shunning—intolerance can be socially destructive. Indeed, said John Stuart Mill, a conformist culture can practice "a social tyranny more formidable than many kinds of political oppression, since, though not usually upheld by such extreme penalties, it leaves fewer means of escape, penetrating much more deeply into the details of life, and enslaving the soul itself."[1] Along with prudence, with which it is deeply intertwined, tolerance is therefore one of the prime virtues of a sane polity (5. Prudence).

At the same time, however, mores constitute the polity. This means that society must uphold a certain standard of behavior and also inculcate a body of shared beliefs (3. Mores the Keystone). If society is too tolerant, if there are no rules that all must obey regardless of personal inclination, then anomie and disintegration are the result. In addition, as Sigmund Freud pointed out in *Civilization and Its Discontents*, repression is the price we pay for civilization. In the end, therefore, the mores of the community must prevail, even though this inflicts suffering on individuals with contrary predilections (2. Community Prior to Individual).

To put it another way, liberty is not an absolute, for otherwise greed and selfishness would run rampant, and the society would soon be destroyed (12. Restrained Liberty). So a prudent balance between freedom and repression, tolerance and conformity, and rights and responsibilities must be struck (13. Civil Rights).

This is not easy in any area of life, but the realm of religious belief and observance is the most difficult. Religion is, after all, a matter of good and evil and of obeying the will of heaven. To accept that others do not see the world in the same way and may even find intolerable certain customs supposedly enjoined by one's religion is hard. But unless the community is homogenous, there is no alternative to requiring believers to tolerate unbelievers and vice versa—in other words, for everyone to compromise for the sake of community harmony. To do otherwise opens the door to a multiplicity of demands for special treatment and eventual balkanization. (For this reason, as set forth in 24. Mosaic Society, organizing multi-ethnic or multi-religious societies by "quarter" can assist in reducing friction between different groups.)

As noted above, prudence and tolerance are twinned virtues. In practice, prudence enjoins not going to extremes and not being fanatical or bloody-minded, but instead seeking a *modus vivendi* between opposing ideals and practices. In the end, it means working with society and human nature as they actually are—flawed, divided, refractory—not as one would like them to be, and then moderating thought and action accordingly, leaving perfection to the angels and seeking imperfect but tolerable solutions that allow us to live at peace.

To achieve this end, hypocrisy is a social necessity. Usually regarded as reprehensible, the vice of hypocrisy is essential precisely because it pays tribute to virtue. Human beings are passionate creatures, but living together requires that their passions be channeled or repressed. Some things have to remain in the closet, or society cannot exist. But as long as individual behavior does not frighten the horses or upset the children —that is, as long as everyone sins discreetly—then at least some of these passions can be acted out behind closed doors between consenting beings without thereby calling into question the standards of the community. Hypocrisy is, therefore, the balm that makes conformity to community standards bearable. We must tolerate what we cannot reasonably regulate or, as Mill said, risk "enslaving the soul itself."

In addition, human life cannot be only Apollonian—all order and reason. Dionysus must have his due, or he will erupt destructively in the famous return of the repressed.[2] This means that there need to be ritualized outlets for the passionate, shadow side of human nature. The Balinese cockfight is one such example. Balinese men, who are forbidden to show any form of anger, discharge their aggression in proxy wars between fighting cocks.[3]

By selectively tolerating what it cannot extinguish, society eases the pain of repression and gives individuals relatively sane channels for the passions that would otherwise threaten to destroy it.

# 7

## Strong Governance

To govern means to exercise sovereign authority—that is, to control and direct the affairs of the polity. For a people to survive, much less thrive, there must be an entity that performs the essential functions of governance—among them, the defense of the realm, the management of external affairs, the provision of public order, the issuance of currency, the establishment of rules for trade, commerce, and industry, and all the other tasks that can be accomplished only by a people acting in common.

Without such higher authority, individuals will tend to behave in ways detrimental to the public good and harmful to their fellow citizens. It is not so much that human beings are not angels. Given a reasonably healthy civil society grounded on good mores, the decent many usually far outnumber the criminal few. But as men and women have individual desires and private wills, they will naturally tend to go their own ways and pursue their own ends with little regard for the common weal. Hence some kind of sovereign authority holding the power to prescribe and proscribe is indispensable.

As the early Americans discovered, the lack of such an authority has serious disadvantages. They replaced the relatively weak Articles of Confederation with a Constitution establishing a central government that was strong but limited—strong in that it had the necessary authority to perform the essential tasks of governance, but limited in that it was modest in both size and ambition. This gave freedom to enterprises and liberty to individuals.

Governance and administration are not the same. The former lays down the rules; the latter applies them. If the rules are few and general, limited to providing a framework within which people can peacefully flourish, then governance entails both little administration and minimal intrusion into private lives. Whereas an ambitious government will inevitably use its power to extend its ambit, creating an oppressive administration that regulates more and more extensively and penetrates more and more deeply into the minutiae of daily life. The result will be a regime that dominates enterprises and tyrannizes individuals.

The maxim "That government is best which governs least" is therefore mistaken if it is taken to mean a weak government that cannot perform its proper functions, for that would lead to dysfunction, if not anarchy. A strong government is, in fact, the linchpin of a society. But the statement is profoundly true if it is taken to mean that government must be limited and small, so that it does not become oppressive or tyrannical (8. Limited Government and 10. Small Administration).

In *On Liberty*, John Stuart Mill shows where the line should be drawn:

> A government cannot have too much of the kind of activity which does not impede, but aids and stimulates, individual exertion and development. The mischief begins when, instead of calling forth the activities and powers of individuals and bodies, it substitutes its own activity for theirs.[1]

If this is government's proper role, then one of its foremost duties is to nurture civil society. For only a strong civil society allows government to be authoritative yet limited. When civil society breaks down for whatever reason, the government is impelled to intervene. This initiates a vicious circle of declining personal independence and responsibility that fuels the rise of an administrative Leviathan.

It follows that the government must be the guardian of the society's mores (3. Mores the Keystone) but without trying to legislate morality (9. Minimal

Laws). Similarly, it has to prevent excessive economic inequality while still allowing individuals and enterprises freedom of activity (23. Rough Equality and 30. Market Regulation).

To summarize, freedom is not the absence of governance. Rather, freedom flourishes only within a framework of rules established and maintained by a strong government. It is the rules that constitute the game and create the possibility of play. But let them be broad and general, leaving the widest possible latitude for Mill's "individual exertion and development."

# 8

## Limited Government

Strong governance does not mean unlimited government. To the contrary, the purpose of strong governance is to create a solid and stable framework of laws and institutions that allows people to pursue their own ends. As Walter Lippmann said, "In a free society the state does not administer the affairs of men. It administers justice among men who conduct their own affairs."[1] Hence governments should not be ambitious. Their job is to facilitate and enable human freedom by establishing good rules and then letting men and women play the game themselves.

But to make a people largely self-governing, as Lippmann desires, takes more than a government content to be an umpire. It also assumes good mores, excellent education, and a citizenry that knows the difference between liberty and license—in other words, a strong civil society (3. Mores the Keystone, 12. Restrained Liberty, and 22. Education for Excellence).

Unless individuals are willing and able to take responsibility for their own lives and also to be content with what their own enterprise and labor bring them, popular irresponsibility and discontent will create a vacuum that sooner or later draws the government into administering the affairs of men and women (10. Small Administration). It follows that a primary function of strong governance is to ensure that government remains limited by nurturing civil society (7. Strong Governance).

Restrained governmental ambition is especially critical in two areas. First, a government cannot make the eradication of vice into a goal. Human beings are imperfect, and the summation of their individual imperfections produces an even more imperfect society in which many varieties of dysfunction and deviance will inevitably take root. Because criminalizing this behavior is costly and futile, the society needs to establish a *modus vivendi* with the innate weakness of humankind (6. Tolerance and 9. Minimal Laws).

Second, to the extent that problems emerge from the free play of men and women, the government's role should be to reform the rules so as to restore free play rather than to achieve some social ideal. For example, it is better to be satisfied with a rough equality rather than insisting that all shall have steak no matter what the cost or, conversely, forcing all to eat beans out of some misguided fixation on "fairness" (23. Rough Equality).

In general, therefore, government must stand above the fray, administering justice among men, as Lippmann enjoins, and resolutely resisting what Alexis de Tocqueville called the dangerous temptation "to enslave men in the minor details of life."[2]

Above all, government must never become the tool of those in thrall to mad schemes to remake the world in accordance with some grand ideal. Human systems, like biological systems, seem to have a natural shape that must be respected. In the human case, it is both possible and necessary to moderate that shape so that the tendency for wealth to accumulate and power to concentrate is checked. Otherwise the game would be over and citizens would no longer be free—and to prevent this outcome is precisely the role and function of government.

But it is not possible or even advisable to remove every inequality, injustice, unfairness, and imperfection. All of history testifies that the attempt to eradicate these and other "evils" will almost certainly create new and worse ones–at an extreme, gulags, reigns of terror, bloody repression, even mass murder. Just as we must learn to accept that men and women will always be a little bit vicious, we must also be content with a society that is only moderately bad and only partially sane. Otherwise we may be visited by massive evil and mass insanity.

# 9

## Minimal Laws

To govern means to control and direct the affairs of the polity. But wise governance is not ambitious. Governments should not be drawn into schemes, such as the welfare state, that engender an oppressive administrative state (10. Small Administration and 23. Rough Equality). For the same reason, they must refrain from making a plethora of laws that necessitate a large and intrusive law enforcement apparatus.

Like government or administration, law enforcement is driven by the iron law of power: the more it has, the more it wants. If this tendency is not firmly checked, the society will more and more resemble a police state.

The Taoist adage, "Multiply laws, multiply criminals," applies. More laws mean more arrests, more trials, and more prisons. And it tends to be a vicious circle in that prisons usually breed worse criminals (35. Graduated Prisons).

Although the first line of defense against crime is a strong civil society of rough equals (3. Mores the Keystone and 23. Rough Equality), there will always be a few who are too crooked or passionate to be their own constables. Laws against murder, rape, kidnapping, robbery, theft, arson, fraud, and all the other felonies are, therefore, unavoidable. No society can exist without them.

Depending on the complexity of the society, other laws will also be necessary—for example, measures to preserve public health and maintain food safety or to prevent stock manipulation and tax evasion. But not everything should be criminalized.

Indeed, there comes a point where society must tolerate what it cannot effectively prohibit. Morality cannot be legislated. Prohibition of various substances and activities has been repeatedly tried and has repeatedly failed. What is worse, the very attempt damages the society. Human nature being what it is, prohibition creates black markets, corruption, mafias, contempt for laws, and other side effects that are completely predictable but that are usually ignored by those avid to stamp out "vice."

Vice cannot be eliminated, only regulated, taxed, and contained after the fashion of Yoshiwara, a walled and guarded pleasure quarter established in Edo (the former name of Tokyo) by the Tokugawa Shogunate of premodern Japan. Thus confined, vice did not contaminate the larger society directly. There were, of course, indirect effects. The laws regulating behavior within the walls maintained order and cleanliness, but individuals were free to drink themselves into a stupor, gamble away the rent money, and in general indulge themselves to the detriment of their persons and families. So Yoshiwara was not a perfect solution, only a better one than having vice scattered around the city, where all these same problems occur but in a less controlled and more insidious fashion. In other words, better a formal zone of tolerance than the alternative.

It may seem hypocritical to allow depravity in one area while strictly forbidding it elsewhere. But such is the human condition: hypocrisy is the vice that, in paying tribute to virtue, actually supports morality (6. Tolerance).

In the end, societies must not strive for more than human beings are capable of. The effort to perfect society is likely to entail worse evil than the evil itself. In addition to the problems mentioned above, it produces a special kind of tyranny condemned by C. S. Lewis:

> Of all tyrannies, a tyranny sincerely exercised for the good of its victims may be the most oppressive. It may be better to live under robber barons than under omnipotent moral busybodies. The robber baron's cruelty may sometimes sleep, his cupidity may at some point be satiated;

but those who torment us for our own good will torment us without end for they do so with the approval of their own conscience.[1]

The attempt to perfect humanity and society by legal means is, therefore, dangerous to liberty. It is a minor manifestation of that worst of all political delusions: that refractory human beings must be remade into new men and women, even if this requires tyranny (7. Limited Government).

# 10

## Small Administration

A strong sovereign authority is essential. It enacts and enforces laws that make it possible to play the social and economic game (7. Strong Governance). But such an authority can also be limited both in its actions and in its aims (8. Limited Government and 9. Minimal Laws). Thus the administrative apparatus of the state (which is what critics of "big government" usually have in mind) can be small and closely confined to the indispensable functions of governance.

In fact, it is the absence of strong governance that creates an overgrown and oppressive administration. A government that is strong is able to assert the public interest over private inclination. It can also take a long view of the common good (15. Long Time Horizon). In contrast, a government that is weak does what is easy and popular, following the line of least resistance and catering to enterprises and individuals even if this is destructive in the long term.

For example, it is certainly easier to pile up debts and then inflate them away than to insist on fiscal probity, even though debasing the currency is known to be suicidal in the long run (28. Pay As You Go and 29. Sound Money). It is also easier to accommodate economic power than to police it, even though a lack of effective regulation engenders destructive booms and busts, fuels the tendency toward monopoly, and progressively impoverishes the majority (30. Market Regulation). Worst of all, yielding to popular desires for welfare or for government to "do something" about some perceived ill sooner or later entails "big government" in the form of an administrative state (23. Rough Equality).

Such an administrative state is an abomination on many levels. First, it soon becomes fiscally insupportable. It therefore induces politicians to debase the currency or to commit other stupidities rather than do the right but difficult thing of checking the expansion of governmental power.

Second, however, an administrative state soon becomes so big and complex that it can no longer be reined in, even if politicians have the courage to do so. It begins to run on its own momentum, to have its own dynamic, to follow its own rationale. In consequence, reform efforts are not only frustrated, but they will usually make matters worse.

Third, an administrative state is a paradise for bureaucrats, lawyers, and accountants and a hell for everyone else (including the above in their private capacity). The simplest thing requires high-priced professional help. A thicket of regulation entangles enterprises, which are forced to spend unproductive time and money for "compliance"—or to engage in more-or-less legal bribery of politicians. Individuals find that they can do nothing—not even own a pet or a bicycle—without a permit or license from some office. With its back to the fiscal wall, the government becomes avid for revenue, so taxes are high and tax collectors exigent. Powerful bureaucracies feather their own nests and warp the political process. In short, administrators and their minions thrive while citizens suffer.

Unfortunately, a government must have power to perform its essential functions. But because power hankers after power, the seemingly inevitable tendency is for it to become concentrated and centralized. Countermeasures that keep governance strictly limited are therefore crucial. Above all, anything that threatens to make the apparatus of administration larger must be strenuously resisted. To the extent that administration is necessary, it should be kept as parsimonious and as local as possible.

To rephrase the classic maxim, "That government is best which governs well but administers least." Otherwise citizens soon become actors in a play written by Franz Kafka.

# 11

## Collective Leadership

As Lord Acton famously said, power tends to corrupt, and absolute power corrupts absolutely. As a corollary, he also maintained that no class is truly fit to govern.[1] But since some class must govern, and to govern is to exercise power, how do we ensure that rulers use power lawfully in the service of the polity?

There can be no final answer to this dilemma; it is simply a given of the human condition. But there are measures that can limit the corruption. Following Montesquieu, the framers of the American Constitution believed that the solution was a separation of powers among the executive, legislative, and judicial branches, so that each could check and balance the other two.

This is certainly an important part of the answer. Unless each branch of government has its own power basis, it risks becoming an instrument of one of the others. For example, without an independent judiciary, a fair trial is impossible. Complaisant or fearful judges will find the president's rivals guilty on trumped-up charges and sentence them to a lengthy sojourn in Siberia. Similarly, a legislature under the executive thumb will be nothing but a rubber stamp.

The right balance is not easy to maintain. Courts can usurp the function of legislatures, and presidents can grow steadily more imperial over time. Hence it is necessary to reassess and perhaps readjust the balance periodically (19. Constitutional Convention).

Moreover, the risk attached to such a balance-of-power system is that the checks are too effective and therefore result in stagnation. Indeed, in the case of the American polity, because the framers were so concerned to prevent potential tyranny, they deliberately created what Richard Hofstadter called "a harmonious system of mutual frustration."[2] Yet from the failure of the Articles of Confederation, the framers also drew the conclusion that effective governance needed a strong executive power, so they created the office of the president.

However, a one-person executive is not an ideal solution for two reasons. First, as mentioned, the office itself tends to grow steadily more powerful over time. Second, duly elected presidents corrupted by the power of the office may cling to it in one way or another, either by creating an unbeatable political machine or by effecting a coup d'état that makes them president-for-life or some other euphemism for autocrat.

It follows that executive power should be exercised collectively. This prevents not only excessive power in the hands of one person but also the intoxicating adulation and poisonous invective often directed at individual leaders. The Swiss joke that no one knows the name of the country's president—a first-among-equals who simply chairs a seven-member federal council for a one-year term—is obviously hyperbole, but it does show that shared executive power can be both modest and effective.

Similarly, in a well functioning parliamentary system, the prime minister is more than first among equals. But he must nevertheless persuade cabinet members and even backbenchers to go along with his policies or face defections and a vote of confidence.

In short, except in extraordinary times that require a suspension of normal politics (18. Constitutional Dictatorship), it is best to make leadership collective. Entrusting power to one class is inescapable; entrusting it to one person is perilous.

# 12

## Restrained Liberty

Liberty is not an absolute. John Locke, the author of the modern liberal tradition, was quite explicit on this point:

> The *Freedom* then of Man and Liberty of acting according to his own Will, is *grounded on* his having *Reason*, which is able to instruct him in that Law he is to govern himself by, and make him know how far he is left to the freedom of his own will. To turn him loose to an unrestrain'd Liberty, before he has Reason to guide him, is not the allowing him the privilege of his Nature, to be free; but to thrust him out amongst Brutes, and abandon him to a state as wretched, and as much beneath that of a Man, as theirs.[1]

Ergo, liberty must be restrained. The American founders made the same point more pithily: liberty is not license.

The fundamental dilemma of human association is that men and women have a surfeit of passion and a deficit of reason. It is the function of government to check the one and supply the other, so that people can live together productively and peacefully.

This means that individuals cannot be allowed to construct a private version of reason that authorizes them to follow their particular will and appetite—like the Marquis de Sade, whose philosophy justified depravity. Or like the Maasai, who believe that since God gave them ownership of all the cows in the world, rustling cattle from their neighbors is not just permissible, but obligatory. In other words, the reason to which Locke refers is a considered, collective judgment on where liberty turns into license.

It is also a fact of collective life that liberties must be balanced against responsibilities and duties. A society consisting of all takers and no givers would not long survive. Likewise, one that failed to uphold basic standards of hygiene would soon be sick in every sense of the word.

So government must restrain individual liberty for the common good. Just how far liberty must be restrained and just what is the common good are fraught questions, and striking the right balance between collective needs and individual rights is therefore far from easy.

However, other patterns provide a framework for decision. For instance, to cite a few of the most relevant, government itself has to be limited and must never be arbitrary (8. Limited Government and 13. Civil Rights); property must be used responsibly and the interests of posterity taken into account (15. Long Time Horizon and 25. Usufruct); and economic activity must be in harmony with nature (1. Nature First and 27. Thermodynamic Economy).

In the end, an unrestrained liberty is a prescription for license and disorder, so a balance has to be struck between the legitimate needs of society and the legitimate desires of citizens. Otherwise, the virtue of liberty turns into the vice of anarchy.

# 13

# Civil Rights

The community may be prior to the individual (2. Community Prior to Individual), but that does not mean that citizens should have only duties and no rights. To the contrary, the predatory tendencies of governments must be firmly and decisively checked. A polity that does not respect a people's desire for dignity and freedom is fundamentally evil and will sooner or later generate popular insanity in the form of apathy, addiction, corruption, and crime. Citizens should enjoy reasonable rights and freedoms, and governments must be strictly limited in how they use their coercive power.

Above all, governance cannot be arbitrary. In ancient Greece, where autocracy was the rule, the distinction between king and tyrant was that the former posted laws in the agora, so that all could know what was permitted and what not. Whereas the tyrant ruled despotically: the law was whatever he said it was. Thus there must be published legal codes so that all can distinguish licit from illicit, and established legal procedures so that all will be treated even-handedly should they run afoul of the law.

Government must also be even-handed in general, which is to say that it should not discriminate by favoring one sect, class, or race over another. And if it sees a particular group being persecuted or unfairly disadvantaged, then it must remedy the situation.

In general, however, governments should be wary of intruding. Dignity requires independence. Government's role is to impose the macro-constraints that make civilized life possible, not to control behavior with micro-constraints that force the citizen into a servile dependency on the state (8. Limited Government and 9. Minimal Laws).

Finally, governments must not be cruel. Torture and the like can never be tolerated. Prison systems should be humane and oriented toward rehabilitation for petty first offenders and sequestration for the truly incorrigible (35. Graduated Prisons).

How these general principles are translated into concrete measures is something each polity must decide for itself. Much depends on context. People living on a sparsely populated frontier can have more freedoms than those living in a crowded city. In addition, reasonable people can differ on particulars—for example, whether the death penalty for heinous crimes is inherently cruel—while still respecting the principle. The point is to ensure that the right spirit of the laws prevails, not to make a fetish of, say, the jury system.

Rights cannot be abstracted from reality or made into absolutes. The individual need for freedom and dignity has to be balanced against the social need for law and order. Thus liberty must be restrained lest it become license, and a market economy must be regulated lest it generate monopoly and other ills (12. Restrained Liberty and 30. Market Regulation).

More generally, asserting individual rights *against* the power of the state is contradictory; civil rights can only exist *within* the order provided by the state. To fixate on an unattainable freedom from all government coercion therefore misses the crucial point articulated by Jean-Jacques Rousseau: "Freedom is found in no form of government; it is in the heart of the free man."[1]

To say this in no way diminishes the importance of civil rights. They are a *sine qua non* of sane polity. But of equal importance is that the polity function well, so that people are able to live their lives constructively and creatively within a community that is civil and law abiding. In the end, there is a deep wisdom in Alexander Pope's famous couplet:

For Forms of Government let fools contest;

Whate'er is best administered is best.

# 14

## Personal Voting

Criticism of democracy began with Plato and has continued ever since. Ironically, in light of later developments, even the American founders opposed it: "Democracies have ever been spectacles of turbulence and contention; have ever been found incompatible with personal security or the rights of property; and have in general been as short in their lives as they have been violent in their deaths," said James Madison in Federalist No. 10.[1] For Jean-Jacques Rousseau, democracy was a beautiful but unattainable ideal: "If there were a people of Gods, it would govern itself democratically. Such a perfect government is not suited to men."[2] And he considered representative democracy based on periodic elections to be a sham.[3] Yet when all is said and done, we are left with Winston Churchill's epitome of a back-handed compliment: "Democracy is the worst form of government except all those other forms that have been tried from time to time."[4]

However, Aristotle's rejoinder to Plato—that citizens are not seamen obliged to follow the captain's orders, but diners authorized to judge the chef's cooking—provides a better starting point for thinking about popular rule.[5] Aristotle favored democracy not just because he thought people had both the capacity and the right to make political decisions, but also because he believed political participation would enhance individual self-development. However, implicit in Aristotle's defense are two essential preconditions for making democracy a reality instead of a travesty.

First, genuine participation in civic life occurs only in relatively small, simple, face-to-face societies in which individuals can enter the arena of politics to see and judge for themselves. By contrast, in a society that is large, complex, remote, and divided, participation becomes purely symbolic. Meaningful democracy therefore requires that individuals have direct access to decision making and direct personal knowledge of matters up for decision.

Second, unless the polity is so simple and local that it fulfills Rousseau's ideal—a gathering of peasants deciding their simple affairs under an oak tree—democracy must, of necessity, be representative. But for voters to elect someone else to serve as their proxy, they should actually know that person. "If the citizens of a state are to judge and to distribute offices according to merit," said Aristotle, "they must know each other's characters; where they do not possess this knowledge, both the election to office and the [administration of justice] will go wrong"[6] People are shrewd judges of character when they live closely with someone, but when their information is secondhand, they are readily bamboozled by demagoguery and imagery. Thus elections will "go wrong" as voters get entangled in the web of mendacity, duplicity, and obfuscation spun by distantly seen candidates. Again, real democracy requires direct personal knowledge: citizens must know firsthand the character of candidates for election.

Mass democracy is, therefore, an oxymoron. In a grandiose setting, democracy invites "turbulence and contention"—that is, an ignorant and impassioned mob fighting over the tiller of the ship of state, just as Plato feared. And it tends to elevate to office those who are most ambitious for power and least scrupulous about wielding it.

A polity therefore confronts an existential dilemma. Thomas Jefferson expressed it as follows: "We must make our election between *economy and liberty*, or *profusion and servitude*."[7] In other words, because genuine democracy requires a simple setting, if the people want a democratic polity, then they must be content with simplicity. But if they desire wealth and complexity, then elections in such a setting will produce a travesty of democracy—a meritocracy of bamboozlers, manipulators, and panderers who pursue their own interests ahead of the people's business.

This argues that democracy not be made into a fetish. Which is more important: that citizens be able to vote on everybody from dogcatcher to president, as well as on ill-considered popular initiatives that usurp legislation, or that the polity function well? Democracy is both desirable and workable at the local level, where participants can (at least in theory) have direct personal knowledge of issues and persons. In this respect, the New England town meeting remains a worthy model. However, above this level, the vices of popular rule begin to outweigh its merits and tend to produce a sham democracy. Above all, it is entirely unreasonable to expect the people at large to make critical decisions on complex technological issues (17. Technology Board) or, in fact, to decide any important issue except when guided by wise leadership and thoughtful reflection (16. Wisdom Council and 21. Natural Aristocracy).[8]

So only a mixed polity–a republican democracy that integrates Plato and Aristotle–can bridge the two horns of the dilemma. Smaller constituencies combined with stricter voter qualifications at the local level, supplemented by indirect elections at higher levels, would support a restrained democracy within a republican superstructure serving as the guarantor of liberty (12. Restrained Liberty and 13. Civil Rights) and also as the seat of stability, continuity, and sagacity (5. Prudence and 6. Tolerance). In short, the American founders laid down a pattern that may yet have much to teach us.

# 15

## Long Time Horizon

To be successful over the long term, a polity must have a long time horizon, husbanding its legacy from the past and preparing a bequest for the future.

Edmund Burke famously argued that the present generation receives the past as patrimony that it holds in entail—that is, with an obligation to respect and preserve what it has received, so that it is transmitted to posterity undiminished (25. Usufruct). Just as children owe an inestimable debt to the parents who raised them, those now living are the beneficiaries of ancestors who built the physical infrastructure of a complex society—homes, farms, factories, businesses, libraries, opera houses, universities, and so forth. Likewise, they inherit all the laws, institutions, and mores that that constitute its social infrastructure. Not to treat this precious legacy with respect, preserving its best features while reforming what needs changing due to altered circumstances, is not only base ingratitude, it is also a path to perdition that undermines and eventually destroys a society physically and morally.

With respect to the future, the rights and interests of posterity have yet to find a defender as eloquent as Burke. Indeed, the opposite attitude—"What has posterity ever done for me?"—is more the rule. Thus the well-being of future generations tends to count for little in the councils of state. In practice, so-called welfare states spend far more on moribund grandparents than on vulnerable grandchildren. But if we rightly condemn parents who selfishly spend down an inheritance, leaving nothing to their children, why can it be right for an entire society to behave likewise? In fact, any society that does not have a project that endures, a vision of a better future toward which the society is moving, is probably condemning itself to spiritual and political poverty.

For the present to have meaning, it must see the past as legacy and the future as bequest. Those who live for the moment only may experience temporary gratification but not genuine satisfaction. In the end, what makes societies great is not conquest or consumption but their dedication to something grander than themselves (4. Guiding Ideal).

To put it another way, genuine well-being, both personal and social, comes from the pursuit of felicity and the striving for excellence. (This is precisely what the American founders' "pursuit of happiness" contemplated; it was never intended to authorize a way of life devoted to mere self-seeking.) It follows that a polity should order its economic life accordingly (26. Economy of Plenitude), and also its educational arrangements and social philosophy (21. Natural Aristocracy and 22. Education for Excellence). Otherwise, it condemns itself to mediocrity in the present and inanity in the future.

# 16

## Wisdom Council

Philosopher-kings being scarce on the ground, a polity must find wisdom elsewhere. Although the purpose of many other patterns is precisely to encourage and institutionalize political and economic wisdom (see, for example, 21. Natural Aristocracy and 29. Sound Money), more is needed.

Those who handle the day-to-day affairs of the polity as executives and legislators will inevitably be preoccupied with their duties and will not have the leisure to reflect deeply on the implications of their actions. They will also face a multitude of political pressures that they must accommodate. Nor are they disinterested. To the contrary, they normally desire to remain in office and trim their sails accordingly. Hence they cannot always be expected to stand up for principle or to be a source of wisdom and virtue for the people at large. It follows that the polity needs a wisdom council, a council of elders that stands above the fray and offers both moral and practical guidance.

This is an ancient institution. All traditional societies had councils of elders in one form or another, and almost all kings had a privy council, a small group of experienced statesmen to provide advice and counsel. Philosophers have urged something similar. In Book XII of *The Laws*, for example, Plato has the Athenian Stranger propose a Nocturnal Council to advise the guardians and to educate and enlighten the populace. Even contemporary academicians devoted to the democratic ideal recognize that popular rule does not always lead to the best outcome, so they propose alternatives that would foster greater wisdom.[1]

How to choose the original members of a wisdom council is a question for which there can be no definite answer, except that it should involve consensus.

Once in existence, however, the incumbents would be responsible for grooming and selecting successors, as is the case with the *Académie Française* and the faculties of elite universities.

The wisdom council would have five functions:

- To serve as guardian of the guiding ideal
- To take the long view
- To advise the government on policies
- To educate the populace
- To propose constitutional reforms

In furtherance of these functions, the wisdom council might convene social juries to deliberate particular issues.[2] Jurors could be selected randomly from the general population or from a panel of qualified individuals (or from both as a way to combine democracy and aristocracy). In addition, the council might find it useful to develop a dedicated corps of inspectors or mandarins specifically trained to assist it in carrying out its duties (and also to be a pool of jurors as above). Finally, the wisdom council would need to work closely with the body responsible for evaluating technology (17. Technology Board).

A well-constituted wisdom council would be more than the sum of its functions. Its charisma would make its decisions and acts authoritative; its prestige would keep the polity true to its principles.

# 17

## Technology Board

Technology is inescapably political. Despite its professed neutrality—"technology is neither good nor bad, only a tool to be used for good or bad ends" goes the usual rationale for *laisser innover*—it has, in fact, become the most powerful actor on the social, economic, political, and geopolitical stages during the past three hundred years.

Consider the radical changes wrought by steam engines, automobiles, aircraft, antibiotics, atomic bombs, televisions, and computers. We live in a world utterly transformed—for the better in many ways, but also for the worse in many others. Any dispassionate appraisal of the impact of technology on humankind would have to agree with Carl Jung:

> We refuse to recognize that everything better is purchased at the price of something worse... [N]ew methods and gadgets...by no means increase the contentment or happiness of people on the whole. Mostly, they are deceptive sweetenings of existence, like speedier communications, which unpleasantly accelerate the tempo of life and leave us with less time than ever before.[1]

These words are not just the grumbling of an old man annoyed by "progress." Something better does indeed make other things worse. The automobile gives us the boon of personal mobility, but the direct price is pollution, injuries, and deaths, and the indirect price includes all the costs and consequences of having a petroleum industry, the loss of good farmland to urban sprawl, the social revolution caused by greater personal mobility, traffic-choked cities friendlier to cars than to people, and thinly disguised resource wars, to mention only some of the most salient. The more powerful the technology, the greater the attendant costs and risks. It is no accident that nuclear power has been called a "Faustian bargain."[2]

Just like *laissez faire*, *laissez innover* is a good servant but a bad master. Change is inevitable, but as with a market economy that cannot mean anything goes (30. Market Regulation). Rapid technological change is especially dangerous, because it destroys the old patterns of life faster than viable new ones can be created. Technology must, therefore, be brought under some semblance of political control, or it will in the end destroy the basis of civil society.

To achieve such control will require a board charged with seeing that technological reason (allied to the profit motive) is not given free rein to run roughshod over the "contentment or happiness of people on the whole." Proponents of technological change wax enthusiastic about the benefits (and profits) that will accrue from innovation, but they are curiously silent about possible negative consequences, especially the long-term ripple effects.

The technology board's role would be to discover all these negatives and then to provoke a debate on whether the good to be expected from a particular innovation outweighs the bad. The burden of proof must always be on the proponents, with no benefit of the doubt allowed. The board should be especially vigilant and rigorous in examining innovations that threaten to create runaway, irreversible changes. A key question would be, "What is the worst that can happen if we allow this to go forward?" For if such a worst-case scenario can be foreseen, it will in most cases eventually become a reality.

Inventions cannot, of course, be uninvented. However, their implementation can be controlled by the polity to minimize the environmental and social costs and maximize the human and social gains. Thus the technology board would conclude its assessment of costs and risks with recommendations for making the invention serve long-term human needs instead of short-term economic gains.

The board might also require innovators to post a bond against the possibility of damaging side effects. As matters stand now, innovators tend to reap most of the gains and to evade most of the costs, which are borne by society. But if they were required to persuade private insurers that their invention was relatively harmless, then at least the riskiest innovations could be screened out.

Like the wisdom council, but even more so, a technology board would need to have a corps of trained specialists. It could also use juries to further its deliberations, but these would have to be drawn either from that same corps or from panels of laymen and women qualified by education and experience to be reasonably competent judges of technology, not from the population at random.[3] In this area, democracy must yield to expertise.[4]

The technology board is not intended to be a reactionary institution opposed on principle to all innovation. To the contrary, its mission is genuinely progressive: to tame technology, so that the inventive genius of humankind engenders prosperity and felicity instead of insanity.

# 18

## Constitutional Dictatorship

No matter how skillfully a polity manages its internal affairs, crises will inevitably impose themselves from the outside. Wars, natural disasters, plagues, famines, and other emergencies can arise that require extraordinary measures and exceptional leadership—that is, a temporary suspension of politics as usual, so that the society can be effectively mobilized to combat the threat. Just as many primitive tribes had a war chief to assume command when conditions required, it would be wise to institutionalize procedures for emergency leadership and action, which would otherwise have to be created *ad hoc* at the worst possible time.[1]

More important, because war is the health of the state, it should not be left in the hands of regular political leaders. For once invoked, the martial spirit tends to perpetuate itself and produce an imperial polity. Likewise, executive powers assumed during emergencies tend to become permanent. But if leadership during wars and other grave emergencies were exercised outside the normal operations of the state, these risks would be lessened, if not eliminated entirely. Having defeated the enemy, Cincinnatus would return to his plow, and normal politics would resume.

It follows that there should be formal criteria and procedures for the establishment of a temporary dictatorship when necessary and for its dissolution once the emergency is over. Thus the polity could confront a crisis with concentrated power and forceful action without thereby undermining either its integrity or its ideals.

# 19

## Constitutional Convention

Thomas Jefferson famously called for a revolution every generation. These radical words embody an essential truth. Decay is an inescapable fact of life, so no matter how scrupulously a polity tries to remain true to its original principles, it is bound to fail. Little by little, corruption and petrifaction creep in, as governments are captured by vested interests and administrations by hidebound bureaucrats. Unless these tendencies are checked at an early stage, they become entrenched. Fundamental change is no longer possible, and attempted reforms only deepen the contradictions (as when a "simplified" tax code of twelve thousand pages replaces one with a mere ten thousand pages).

In addition, social, economic, material, geopolitical, and, above all, technological change is incessant. The polity must find a way to remain true to its principles while still accommodating this changing world.

The solution is not a revolution every generation but instead a periodic convention charged with reconstituting the polity. Convened every twenty or twenty-five years, a select group of eminently qualified citizens, guided by the recommendations of the wisdom council and insulated as much as possible from partisan politics, should examine the state of the polity in relation to its constituting patterns. To the extent that it has departed from them, this collective Solon would then mandate measures to bring it back into compliance with its founding ideals, while at the same time adapting the polity to the current state of the world.

In the absence of such a periodic reconstitution, *ad hoc* legislation tainted by partisan or economic interest—precisely the kinds of "reforms" that tend to make matters worse—will proliferate and spread corruption. Or, just as bad, the legal opinions of judges who decide particular cases on narrow grounds according to binding precedent will begin to hogtie the polity. In short, neither legislatures nor judges can be counted on to perform the function of a constitutional convention—to take a considered, long-term view of the best interests of the polity as a whole and then effect the required changes.

Eventually, of course, entropy is bound to prevail, so the polity as originally constituted will no longer exist. But a periodic constitutional convention should at least guarantee that it would not perish through mere oversight.

# 20

## *Paideia*

Just as the polity needs charisma to be stable and legitimate (4. Guiding Ideal), a society must have a higher purpose to be vibrant and healthy. Unless men and women are inspired by some notion of the good life, they will not reach their full potential—and this has political consequences, because unfulfilled and unhappy people will make trouble. In other words, without embracing what the ancients called *paideia*, the society may survive, but it will not thrive.

*Paideia* was defined by Werner Jaeger as "the process of educating man into his true form, the real and genuine human nature."[1] So it is education in the highest sense—education for excellence, character, statesmanship, aesthetic appreciation, and spiritual understanding. In other words, education designed to make not just informed citizens but also wise souls.

Although the school system is obviously inextricably involved in *paideia* (22. Education for Excellence), making citizens and souls ultimately depends on whether the society provides what men and women need to grow into "the real and genuine human nature."

Anticipating the famous formula of Sigmund Freud, Leo Tolstoy wrote, "One can live magnificently in this world if one knows how to work and how to love."[2] And this is profoundly true as far as it goes. Without ties of affection to at least a small circle of intimates, along with a general love of life, an individual is condemned to a barren and lonely existence. Similarly, without meaningful work, life is likely to seem empty and purposeless. The work need not be grand, only suited to the individual's talents. What is important is that it be taken seriously and be seen as a contribution. As Martin Luther King expressed it,

If a man is called to be a street sweeper, he should sweep streets as Michelangelo painted, or Beethoven composed music, or Shakespeare wrote poetry. He should sweep streets so well that all the hosts of heaven and earth will pause to say, "Here lives a great street sweeper who did his job well."[3]

*Paideia* begins in love and work, but it ends in play and prayer. By play is meant the myriad forms of physical and mental culture—that is, all the ways in which human beings can exercise body and mind to bring joy and health. The operative word is *exercise*; mere passive consumption brings little or no benefit.

By prayer is meant any means of spiritual growth, whether this consists of formal religious observance, one of the many yogic practices, or simply private contemplation. As Carl Jung said, "The decisive question for man is: Is he related to the infinite or not?"[4] For if not, then a life of quiet desperation looms, whereas to be related to the infinite brings strength to meet the vicissitudes and ultimate finitude of life with calm and grace.

# 21

## Natural Aristocracy

The cream rises to the top. Rather than denying reality, a wise polity will make this inexorable tendency work to its advantage. In other words, since elites are foreordained, we should bend our efforts not toward frustrating them but instead toward ensuring that they serve the best interests of society. This is especially important in politics, which is necessarily oligarchic in any complex civilization.

Although it has acquired negative connotations in recent times, the original and true meaning of *elite* is "the best or most skilled members of a given group." Thus there are elite sprinters and elite scholars. This does not by itself cause a problem. Everyone understands that only a relative few can win an Olympic gold medal or a Nobel Prize. Indeed, most admire such excellence.

Elite inevitability only becomes a political problem when those at the top form a dominating and corrupt oligarchy that exploits others and monopolizes opportunity, for then the polity becomes a kind of racket. The challenge is, therefore, to foster a genuine elite: a natural aristocracy of talents and virtues, to borrow the formulation of Thomas Jefferson.

A political elite is not only foreordained, it is also necessary if a society is to thrive. No one wants an incompetent pilot at the controls or a bumbling electrician wiring a house for conflagration. Even the most democratic polity would be well advised to ensure that its affairs are directed by those who truly are the best and brightest—that is, not just meritocratic technicians, but genuine statesmen who will not only govern effectively but who will also ennoble politics by appealing to the better angels of our nature instead of our selfish passions. Only thus can individuals and groups be persuaded to make the short-term sacrifices that will bring an abundance of long-term benefits (15. Long Time Horizon).

In modern times, aristocracy is denigrated and meritocracy celebrated, but this has the matter backward. A meritocracy adds value to society but not character—and in the long run, it is character (or, in the older usage, virtue in the form of prudence, discipline, and forethought) that matters if the polity is to survive and also stay true to its principles. On the other hand, a hereditary aristocracy of wealth and birth may add luster to society and has often produced great leaders but at the price of excluding, if not oppressing, the many. A natural aristocracy properly constituted strikes a balance between the two: excellence with openness, merit with character, oligarchy without oppression.

James Madison captured the challenge in these words: "The aim of every political constitution is, or ought to be, first to obtain for rulers men who possess most wisdom to discern, and most virtue to pursue, the common good of the society; and in the next place, to take the most effectual precautions for keeping them virtuous whilst they continue to hold their public trust."[1]

Achieving Madison's two desiderata is not easy, but it is not impossible. Wisdom and virtue are a function of the educational system (22. Education for Excellence), as well as the society's ethos (3. Mores the Keystone). The effectual precautions are that no one person be given exclusive power (11. Collective Leadership) and that the people be secure from arbitrary rule (13. Civil Rights), except when dire circumstances require the suspension of politics as usual (18. Constitutional Dictatorship). If these patterns are well implemented, then a natural aristocracy can guide a polity without compromising liberty and equality.[2]

# 22

---

# Education for Excellence

If there is to be excellence in the polity, there must also be excellence in education. Indeed, the only way to reconcile political excellence with social equality is if the education system fosters virtue and talent instead of entrenching wealth and birth (21. Natural Aristocracy).[1]

The point is not to foster social mobility for its own sake. The brute fact is that talent, however defined, is not uniformly or equally distributed. By definition, half the population is below average on whatever dimension one cares to measure. Hence only the determined and able few can expect to rise in society.

However, this is only a problem if the society fails to acknowledge—and educate for—excellence in its many dimensions. Not every little boy or girl has the potential to be president, but almost all possess some intrinsic talent that education can develop. Thus equipped, they can find a place in society that accords with their abilities and that brings them personal fulfillment as well as recognition from their fellows.

To reiterate, the problem with meritocracy is threefold. First, by exalting talent while neglecting character, it produces a pseudo-elite interested primarily in its own success. Second, it trains the few to succeed in the cutthroat competition to climb a few greasy poles—the ones that command the polity, economy, and society—while consigning the many whose talents lie in other directions to a relative oblivion. Third, those who reach the commanding heights can usually provide their offspring with so many advantages that a meritocracy tends to be self-perpetuating.

The solution is the very opposite of a purportedly democratic one-size-fits-all educational system that institutionalizes mediocrity. Schools should not be places that inculcate a common curriculum pitched to the average, boring the bright and bewildering the backward. Although everyone must learn certain basics, they need not learn it in the same way or at the same pace.

In fact, students should be tracked from the very outset, not to separate sheep from goats, but to determine their learning styles and capacities, so that they can be placed in the most appropriate classrooms. At the same time, students must be closely observed to discover as early as possible wherein lies their unique excellence, so that they can be channeled accordingly. Instead of one big common escalator suiting only a few, there would, therefore, be many smaller escalators, or even little ladders, fitted to the talents and character of each student.

In this way, the man born to play the trumpet and the woman born to observe the stars would be equally happy, equally fulfilled. Provided that the polity was reasonably just, roughly equal, and uniformly civil, why would they care that others made more money or possessed more power?

# 23

## Rough Equality

Because human beings differ greatly in talent and motivation, wealth tends naturally and inevitably to concentrate itself in fewer hands. Unless this tendency for the rich to get richer and the poor poorer is moderated or prevented by peaceful means, it will eventually be remedied by more violent ones. The foremost task of good governance, says Wendell Berry, is, therefore, to protect "the small and weak from the great and powerful."[1]

There are two bad ways to tackle the problem of economic inequality. The first is to place the means of production in the hands of the state, so that it owns and runs the economy instead of merely regulating it. But expropriating the little monopolists to make one big monopolist is no solution. It creates a tyranny that makes all but the ruling clique equally poor and equally subservient. Economic stagnation, social decay, and moral decline are the almost-inevitable result. The means of production must remain in the hands of the people themselves, not arrogated by a state that falsely claims to act in their name.

The second mistake is to allow extensive inequality to develop and then to try to relieve the worst symptoms with a welfare state. As Berry puts it, this is to make the government into "the profligate ineffectual parent of the small and weak after it has permitted the great and powerful to make them helpless."[2]

No matter how healthy a society, there will always be some who fall through the cracks and require temporary assistance or even permanent care. If the numbers are small, then families, charities, and local institutions can cope. However, if the numbers are large, the state is lured into providing a "safety net." This seems reasonable and humane on its face, but once the principle of state responsibility for individual welfare is established, governments are inexorably drawn into providing more and more benefits to more and more people.

Thus personal responsibility continually declines, and dependency on the state continually increases. The terminus of this vicious circle is a demoralized population, a bloated bureaucracy, and a monstrous fiscal burden. In the end, a welfare state turns into a glorified dole and an administrative tyranny. It is not a cure for economic inequality; it is at best a palliative, but one that costs too much and that eventually kills the patient.

Inequality, *per se*, is not the essential problem. Nor can it be prevented entirely without stifling the talented and motivated few whose enterprise and initiative bring economic and social gains to the society. The polity must strike a balance between freedom and control by limiting *laissez faire* so that society realizes its economic benefits without suffering its social costs.[3]

This means that market economies must be regulated to keep them competitive, transparent, and honest (30. Market Regulation). Then those who profit by exploiting the commons must also pay for the privilege, so that fortunes are not founded on mere expropriation (24. Usufruct, 32. Use Tax, and 33. Severance Tax). Finally, those who benefit most from the existence of a free and fair market economy must support the society that enables their good fortune (31. Tax for Revenue and 34. Wealth Tax).

In the end, however, the best defense against inordinate inequality resides in the basic ethos of the society and in institutions that encourage everyone to flourish, not just the "sophisters, economists, and calculators" excoriated by Edmund Burke.[4] Provided the polity embraces aristocratic rather than plutocratic values (21. Natural Aristocracy and 22. Education for Excellence) and fosters an economy as if people mattered (26. Economy of Plenitude), then economic inequality will remain within reasonable bounds and not have harmful social or political consequences.

The true antidote to concentrated wealth is a rich and satisfying culture—for if people do not feel deprived, impoverished, exploited, or disempowered by the great and powerful, economic inequality ceases to be a salient problem. Not everyone will have steak, much less caviar, but they will not lack for beans. To ask more than this—to demand steak for all—is to overreach. The alternative to a rough equality is a tyranny whose solution to the problem of inequality will most likely be beans for all but the favored few.

# 24

## Mosaic Society

Birds of a feather do indeed flock together, and many traditional societies divided cities and towns into quarters inhabited by a particular occupational, ethnic, or religious group. Weavers, Armenians, Zoroastrians, and the like congregated in one area. At the same time, all these groups mingled in the markets, squares, and parks of the city.

This kind of segregation has acquired a bad name in modern times—and, according to John Stuart Mill, it does carry an associated risk:

> Free institutions are next to impossible in a country made up of different nationalities. Among a people without fellow-feeling, especially if they read and speak different languages, the united public opinion necessary to the working of representative government cannot exist.[1]

But in a multicultural society that is divided along racial, ethnic, religious, and social lines, it may nevertheless be useful to allow each group to live according to its own precepts and preferences without thereby provoking friction with other groups. It is much easier for us to tolerate the other if we do not have to deal with his outlandish beliefs, strange behavior, and obnoxious customs day in and day out (6. Tolerance).

In addition, such a system can assist the cause of limited government by devolving certain functions and services to the local level—for example, making each little community responsible for its own cleanliness, having local magistrates deal with minor infractions and disputes, or establishing local dispensaries as an alternative to a distant central clinic.

Of course, allowing groups their own quarter of the city should not exempt them from the laws and mores of the larger community, nor from respecting established civil rights (13. Civil Rights). And a language in common is indeed indispensable. But a mosaic society would give each group a home base from which to participate in and contribute to the larger culture, which can thus reap the benefits of greater diversity without the disadvantages that accompany a nonhomogenous society.

Indeed, a mosaic society is not just a reluctant accommodation to the innate polytheism of humankind; it is desirable in its own right. A homogenous society may be easier to govern, but excessive uniformity or stifling conformity is a recipe for cultural stagnation. Progress in the intellectual, artistic, and spiritual spheres is promoted by competition, cross-fertilization, and cooperation among different social units and personal viewpoints. Just as in the biological realm, therefore, cultural diversity contributes to the richness and resilience of society. In short, better a mosaic than a monoculture.[2]

# 25

---

# Usufruct

The earth belongs to the living, said Thomas Jefferson, but only as life tenants: the current generation has no right to "eat up the usufruct of the lands for several generations to come."[1] At our departure we must leave the earth at least as good a home for humanity as we found it upon arrival.

Usufruct means using resources in such a way that they are not injured or diminished, thereby impoverishing posterity. In practice, however, it involves more than a grudging recognition of the rights of future generations. It implies instead a willingness to plant trees even though we ourselves will never pick the fruit or enjoy the shade. Usufruct entails a policy of stewardship that factors the needs of both the earth and posterity into every economic decision, so that we depart this mortal coil as givers rather than takers.

Hence usufruct has a deep moral significance. It obliges us to restrain appetite not just as a practical matter but because we understand the political truth articulated by Jean-Jacques Rousseau: "For the impulse of appetite alone is slavery, and obedience to the law one has prescribed for oneself is freedom."[2] Usufruct expresses in practical terms the core ideal of a sane polity. The true purpose of political association is to foster character, not consumption (4. Guiding Ideal and 20. *Paideia*).

Although the principle of usufruct should inform decisions of every kind and at all levels, it needs to be supported by practical measures that make a policy of stewardship effective. Above all, economic theory and practice must be rooted in physical reality, so that the ecological and social costs, not just the monetary costs, of human activities are factored into decisions

(27. Thermodynamic Economy). To put it another way, it means to cease treating the earth and its resources as if they were free goods. To this end, a tax regime that makes individuals and entities pay for their use of the commons would be the necessary means for institutionalizing the principle of usufruct (32. Use Tax and 33. Severance Tax).

Usufruct does not entail communism. Individuals may still have personal property, and they may still enjoy the fruits of their labor for the duration of their tenancy, but they cannot possess the earth or any portion of it with the right to exploit it or dispose of it as they see fit. The land was before the community, and the community must see to its preservation.

# 26

## Economy of Plenitude

An economy that aspires to grow constantly bigger, to accumulate more and more wealth, and to operate with greater and greater speed and efficiency will soon encounter the hard truth articulated earlier by Jung: "everything better is purchased at the price of something worse."[1]

In other words, the relentless pursuit of bigger, more, and greater does not necessarily make us better off on balance, because these things entail inescapable trade-offs and sacrifices. Speed and efficiency paradoxically eat up time, excessive wealth can be a curse that consumes nature and corrupts man, and bigness can overwhelm instead of benefit. As Adam Smith noted at the outset of modern political economy, workers paid a price for the "opulence" created by factory production: "All the nobler parts of the human character may be, in a great measure, obliterated and extinguished in the great body of the people."[2]

A critical question is, therefore: What is the economy for? Is it for maximizing personal wealth and national power, which almost always seems to mean maximizing the wealth and power of certain persons and classes, not to mention the state itself? Or is it for humane ends—"Economics as if people mattered," to use E. F. Schumacher's trenchant phrase?[3]

Making the latter election need not involve exchanging *laissez faire* for a stifling command economy that effectively enslaves the populace while falsely claiming to act in its interest. Rather, it requires fostering plenitude—a state of abundance that is just enough to attain essential human ends. To be specific, an economics as if people mattered would be characterized by frugality, sufficiency, amenity, and leisure.

Frugality is the art of making as little as possible go as far as possible—not out of stinginess but as the necessary means for harmonizing an economy with the laws of nature and for ensuring that property and resources are preserved for posterity. So an economy of plenitude will husband precious, limited matter and energy with extraordinary care and will employ labor-intensive production methods allied to intermediate technologies to create ecologically benign goods that have a high use value (24. Usufruct and 27. Thermodynamic Economy).[4]

Sufficiency means to strike a balance between destitution and affluence. Mere subsistence—living hand to mouth—is precarious and demeaning. On the other hand, a surfeit of goods seems to add little to human happiness (and may, in fact, detract from it). There is a place of simplicity in between where there is just enough economic abundance to support a good life for the society as a whole.

One element of this good life is amenity—and primarily public, rather than private, amenity. That is, an economy of plenitude characterized by frugality and sufficiency would feature public swimming pools rather than pools in every backyard—and not only pools, parks, playgrounds, markets, and other common facilities, but also beautiful buildings, convivial streets, and pleasant plazas that make life more interesting and delightful.

Traditional societies can be the model. Individuals may have been poor by modern standards, but they enjoyed civilized environments that put to shame societies marked by private affluence and public squalor. To put it another way, a rich culture does not require having more material goods, but instead using the available goods for worthier ends.

An economy of plenitude would also provide the leisure necessary for human beings to develop themselves to the fullest extent of their talents and interests. Unless economic life is structured to provide an abundance of time, it will engender wage slavery for the many and a rat race for the few. Leisure is the *sine qua non* for *paideia*. If people only work, then time for love, play, and prayer—the requisites for a full human life—will be lacking (20. *Paideia*).

Finally, an economy of plenitude is important for a sane politics.[5] Bigness, wealth, complexity, luxury, haste, and efficiency create the conditions, if not the necessity, for a government that is big, powerful, bureaucratic, expensive, and overbearing.[6] To reiterate the words of Thomas Jefferson, the choice is "between *economy and liberty*, or *profusion and servitude*."[7] In the economic sphere, as in the political, self-restraint is the price of a good life. When limited resources are husbanded to create amenity and beauty–along with the leisure to enjoy them–less can paradoxically be more.

# 27

## Thermodynamic Economy

The human economy is an elaborate machine for converting natural resources into useful goods. It is, therefore, a physical process bound by physical laws—above all, the laws of thermodynamics that govern all transformations of matter and energy.

This brute fact tends to be overlooked in economies in which much, or even most, of the activity is purely financial. At bottom, a currency is simply a means for tracking matter-energy transactions. That is, it is a counter for physical reality, not that reality itself. But the human mind's propensity for misplaced concreteness disposes us to see money as somehow real. This is especially true when credit or inflation expands the money supply out of all proportion to the underlying physical reality, for then the counters turn into abstractions almost entirely divorced from the underlying matter and energy (29. Sound Money).

This failure to ground economies in physical reality causes numerous problems. Toxic wastes are dumped in the environment, renewable resources are overexploited, and nonrenewable resources are consumed instead of invested (1. Nature First and 33. Severance Tax). To avoid ecological self-destruction and make human economies viable over the long term, there must be an accounting system that incorporates all the relevant costs of economic activities, not just monetary prices, into decision making.

As it stands, man keeps one set of books, nature another, and they are not compatible. To accomplish a reconciliation of these two very different ways of accounting will be extremely challenging in practice, but thermodynamics provides the theoretical basis for making the human economy conform to the laws governing the natural economy.

Matter-energy transformations are inherently inefficient. When coal is converted into electricity, more than half of the energy in the coal goes to waste, and transmission losses consume part of the rest. What remains does the work (and is then dissipated into the environment as low-grade heat). So the process is only about 35 percent efficient. We get one good—the electricity—but we create roughly two bads (or three, if we include the low-grade heat). And we have still not counted the energetic cost of mining and transporting the coal, building and maintaining power plants and transmission lines, wiring homes, or manufacturing electric devices, to mention only the direct costs of generating and using electricity. In effect, therefore, nature taxes matter-energy conversions at ruthlessly high rates—over 90 percent in some cases. [1]

The thermodynamic tax can be swept under the carpet for some time—especially if energy is cheap, abundant, and dense, for then it is possible to overpower nature temporarily. Ultimately, however, this strategy encounters diminishing returns; the economy has to run harder and harder just to stay in the same place and eventually collapses. [2] So the postponed tax has to be paid one way or another, and the longer payment is delayed, the more painful the final reckoning.

An economy that accounts for and pays the tax directly and immediately is the only viable, long-term solution. (To use systems language, a healthy economy requires negative feedback loops to keep it in homeostatic balance; otherwise, positive feedback will drive it toward self-destruction.) Such an economy would have the following characteristics:

First, natural capital has to be scrupulously conserved. The human economy must be designed to live on the income from that capital, not on the capital itself, and nothing can be allowed to contaminate or damage the source of the income.

Second, it follows that the economic goal is to minimize thermodynamic costs, not maximize short-term monetary gains, for this is the only way to prosper over the long term. If this means using draft horses instead of tractors, or sailing ships instead of steamships, so be it.

Third, this points toward an economics that is physiocratic, meaning that the basis of value is nature, not labor. The way to transform scarce matter and energy into products with high use value is with human sweat and skill. Hence a thermodynamic economy will be labor intensive and resource conservative.

Fourth, such an economy cannot rely on food, materials, and fuel brought from the ends of the earth but must instead operate with local resources. For the most part, these resources will be diffuse, not concentrated. A thermodynamic economy, therefore, has to be simpler, smaller in scale, mostly decentralized, and perhaps even predominately rural-agrarian.

Fifth, however, this need not entail technological regress. In fact, it will require both an ultra-sophisticated technology that conserves matter and energy and harmonizes with nature and an "intermediate technology" that is more advanced than premodern technologies but also simpler, thermodynamically cheaper, and much less harmful to nature than the technologies of the fossil-fuel era.[3] If there are sailing ships, they might seem both familiar and miraculous to a seaman from the age of clipper ships.

As these broad measures indicate, a thermodynamic economy is much more than a grudging accommodation of human wants to physical reality. Rather, it is the necessary foundation for an "economics as if people mattered" (26. Economy of Plenitude).[4]

# 28

## Pay As You Go

Micawber's iron law of economics states, "Annual income twenty pounds, annual expenditure nineteen pounds nineteen and six, result happiness. Annual income twenty pounds, annual expenditure twenty pounds ought and six, result misery." Mr. Micawber's advice to David Copperfield is just as true for the big household of the state as it is for all the little households that compose it. A state can get away with living beyond its means for some time, but only by dishonest and underhanded means that lead inexorably on to moral and fiscal bankruptcy and, therefore, to mass misery (29. Sound Money).

This does not mean that governments should never use credit. They need bridge loans to manage their finances—that is, temporary borrowing to smooth out fluctuations in income and outgo. As long as debts do not accumulate and governments pay their bills on time, this causes no problems.

Governments also need to invest in physical and social infrastructure, spending money now for benefits later. So they must sell bonds to finance roads, ports, and the like. Again, this is not a problem provided that the investment is useful and that income is available to amortize the debt (32. Use Tax).

However, problems arise when governments and legislatures enact entitlement programs for which they have no actuarially sound payment plans. Or when they issue bonds to build bridges to nowhere or other boondoggles that subtract instead of add value to the society. Or, worse, when they use credit to cover routine expenses. Or, worst of all, when they pay the interest on previous debt by issuing new debt, which is tantamount to a Ponzi scheme.

Unfortunately, the temptation is to do all of the above. After all, it is the government that makes the rules, keeps the books, and issues the currency, so there is no one to call them to account. The problem is especially acute in democracies, where elections are advance auctions conducted by politicians promising something for nothing. It is just so much more convenient to, in the immortal words of the famous advertising campaign, "Fly Now, Pay Later" and stick posterity with the tab. But the eventual and inevitable result of such a policy is misery.

Polities have to obey Micawber's law. Any proposal to spend money must set aside the funds needed to pay for it, either by cutting expenditures elsewhere or by charging fees or by raising taxes. And programs have to be monitored to ensure that expenditures do not grow faster than available income. There is no other way. Governments cannot be allowed to conduct their finances in ways that would be illegal for businesses and ruinous for families. Otherwise, the society will soon join Mr. Micawber in being "floored."

The state's external balance of payments is less easily managed and inevitably subject to fluctuations, but the same principle applies. A state cannot be a perpetual debtor without serious consequences. Nor can it expect to be a perpetual creditor as a matter of policy without inviting enmity and possible retaliation. Economic policy must be managed accordingly.

In short, in ordinary times, a state must neither a borrower nor a lender be, but instead balance income and outgo in both its internal and external accounts. Of course, in extraordinary times, the normal rules may need to be suspended for the duration (18. Constitutional Dictatorship). Once the emergency is over, however, one of the polity's first priorities should be to pay down any accumulated debts and thereafter live again within its means, just as Mr. Micawber enjoins.

# 29

## Sound Money

There is almost universal agreement that inflation destroys a polity.[1] John Maynard Keynes summarized this lesson of history by saying,

> There is no subtler, no surer means of overturning the existing basis of society than to debauch the currency. The process engages all the hidden forces of economic law on the side of destruction, and it does it in a manner which not one man in a million is able to diagnose.[2]

Debauching the currency destroys a society in three ways. First, when no one can predict future values, it upsets the relationship between lenders and borrowers that is the foundation of a capitalist economy. The result is loose credit, misallocation of capital, and speculative excess as individuals struggle to survive and profit in a climate of pervasive uncertainty.

Second, the effect of an inflationary policy, however implemented, is to plunder ordinary citizens. Their accumulated savings become increasingly worthless, so they stop saving and start consuming. But because wages lag the increase in prices, consuming more makes them poorer. Thus the many are progressively impoverished at the same time that the financial casino enriches the few.

Third, on top of growing economic hardship, people see that inflation punishes prudence and thrift while rewarding their opposites. Since virtue no longer pays, they are demoralized and behave accordingly. Individual morality declines, often quite markedly. What is worse, when they realize that their own government is systematically and underhandedly impoverishing them, they feel betrayed and lose all faith in the system, so the social contract is broken.

That debauching the currency would produce a moral debacle is hardly surprising. The phrase *sound money* is practically synonymous with economic stability and good government as well as the virtues of prudence, honesty, foresight, and self-restraint—in other words, the essential qualities of a good society, both practically and morally (5. Prudence).[3]

Many items have served as money over the eons—cowry shells, wampum, peppercorns, even large stones. However, for most of recorded history, sound money has meant gold and silver. Partly this reflects the relative scarcity, perceived beauty, and chemical nobility of these metals. More important, however, they fulfill all of the desiderata for a good form of money, which needs to be simultaneously a medium of exchange, a unit of account, and a store of value: gold and silver are durable, portable, divisible, fungible, and possess intrinsic value. By contrast, land may be durable and valuable, but it is neither portable nor readily divisible. Similarly, commodities like wheat or oil fail one or more of the above tests.

However, gold and silver have drawbacks of their own. Once economic development reaches a certain level, they are simply not as convenient as paper currency. And their very scarcity becomes a limitation, in that a lack of specie can stifle commerce and limit economic growth. Almost all contemporary economists have, therefore, followed Keynes in declaring gold a "barbarous relic" and in anathematizing a return to the gold standard.

Unfortunately, when currencies are not anchored in physical reality and can be created at will, central bankers are bound to bungle the job of managing an economy. They simply do not possess the requisite knowledge to bend a complex system to their will, and they are eternally tempted to print money rather than enforce monetary discipline. In consequence, cutting currencies loose from any tangible standard (as when a banknote can be exchanged for so many grams of gold or silver) will eventually provoke serious problems—credit bubbles and speculative frenzies, followed by spectacular crashes.

In the end, so-called fiat currencies are supported by nothing but confidence. So a policy of inflation may foment an artificial prosperity for a while, but once confidence wanes, once ordinary citizens spot the swindle, such a currency will regress to its intrinsic value—namely, zero. The regression may be slow or swift, but it is certain.

Of course, any currency, whether cowry shells or gold ducats, rests ultimately on confidence—that is, on a tacit agreement that it possesses real value. It is noteworthy that when a currency regime collapses in the aftermath of war, hyperinflation, or social breakdown, a substitute currency immediately arises—most commonly, alcohol and cigarettes, but also bars of soap, rolls of toilet paper, and other useful goods that have obvious worth. By contrast, a fiat currency is said to be created "out of thin air," so it is grounded on nothing and provides no objective basis for confidence.

The upshot is that sound money must be based on a standard of some kind—one that inspires confidence that the currency is indeed worth what it says, both now and in the future. If gold and silver alone are no longer adequate for the purpose, which may be the case, then something else must be found—a basket of precious and industrial metals, a claim on commodities or farmland, a right to a certain quantum of energy, or whatever other sophisticated wampum the human brain can devise. For otherwise, "all the hidden forces of economic law" will conspire to overturn "the existing basis of society."

# 30

---

# Market Regulation

So-called free markets are created and maintained by governments. Markets themselves have existed from time immemorial, but a market economy came into being only when the early modern state established the legal framework necessary for its functioning.[1] And continued supervision by the state is necessary, for without agreed and enforceable rules, economic life would be a war of all against all.

The doctrine of *laissez faire* has to be understood in this context. It urges governments to support private enterprise, because it leads, as Adam Smith said, to "the wealth of nations." History has proven Smith's case. Unlike a command economy run by bureaucrats, the invisible hand of the market does indeed produce "opulence."

But *laissez faire* cannot mean anything goes (see also 17. Technology Board regarding *laissez innover*), and it is certainly not a license for predatory behavior. Nor does it authorize a market economy to dominate the polity, for that is to turn a useful and necessary servant of society into its master (7. Strong Government).

As Robert Kuttner points out, the success of a market economy depends on nonmarket values: "Norms of civility are a public good. Without them the world would degenerate into a society of relentless mutual suspicion"—in other words, a "dystopia."[2] Like personal liberty, therefore, economic freedom must be restrained so that it serves society instead of destroying it (12. Restrained Liberty).

Economic actors will inevitably chafe at the restrictions under which they are forced to operate. But rules that promote honesty, transparency, fair dealing, and employee welfare are essential because capitalism contains two intrinsic moral hazards.

First, observing safety standards, following generally accepted accounting principles, providing benefits, and the like, is burdensome and cuts into profits. Thus economic actors are constantly tempted to cut corners, if not to commit fraud.

Second, competition is bound to lead to a race to the bottom unless owners and managers are prevented from doing what early capitalists did—adulterate products, employ children as pit ponies, dump poisons into drinking water, corner markets, and so on.

That financial scandals and industrial accidents and abuses are a staple media item indicates that these are not trivial concerns. Unless a market economy is well regulated, bad things happen.

Unfortunately, it is also true that too much regulation or the wrong kind of regulation can saddle enterprise with red tape and unwarranted costs—as well as obligations that, however well intended, frustrate business activity or create perverse incentives. For example, by making it too expensive and onerous to hire and fire, so proprietors either do not hire at all or hire only part-timers who work for low wages, receive no benefits, and can be fired peremptorily. Or by imposing rent controls, so landlords skimp on maintenance and refrain from building new apartments. Regulation has to be carefully crafted to make sure that it prevents malfeasance without frustrating enterprise.

This being said, the opposite and equal risk is inadequate regulation due to the phenomenon of regulatory capture, whereby powerful industries use economic clout to bend legislatures and agencies to their will. In effect, business writes the rules by which it will be governed, so it is only after the fact, when there is an incident, that we learn the rules were too lax—that banks engaged in dubious transactions, failed to maintain sufficient reserves, loaned money to people who could not be expected to pay it back, and the like.

Regulating a market economy is, therefore, far from easy or straightforward. As in other areas of polity, the aim is balance: regulating with a firm yet light hand that makes market participants toe the line but that does not stifle entrepreneurship or distort markets.

Unfortunately, not only do governments struggle to find this happy medium, but they are also prone to rig the market instead of regulating it. In effect, bad politics trumps good policy. So politicians actively tilt the economic field to favor this interest or that. Or they make credit too easy because the resulting artificial prosperity improves their chances for reelection. Or they burden enterprise with heavy social obligations, shoving the cost of public programs off onto private parties. Or they abuse the tax system (31. Tax for Revenue). In other words, instead of making the rules of the game and serving as impartial umpires, governments are often fatally tempted to enter the fray themselves and thereby bring about the "mischief" lamented by Mill (7. Strong Governance).

This temptation must be vigorously resisted. For when government goes beyond setting and enforcing general rules and intrudes too deeply into the functioning of the economy, it becomes a giant strangler fig that slowly squeezes the life out of the economic forest.

# 31

## Tax For Revenue

Received wisdom tells us that taxes are the price we pay for a civilized society and that the art of taxation consists in plucking the most feathers with the least amount of hissing from the goose. It follows that revenue should be raised as simply, fairly, efficiently, dispassionately, inexpensively, transparently, and painlessly as possible—all of which would seem to be so patently obvious as to require no justification. Who would deliberately set out to create a tax system that was its exact opposite? Unfortunately, when it is forgotten that the sole purpose of taxation is to raise revenue to support civilized society, then all manner of mischief ensues.

Social engineering via the tax code rigs the system in favor of one interest or another by subsidizing particular groups, classes, professions, and activities. This inevitably leads to taxation becoming a political football and also to a piling up of exceptions, loopholes, and complexities. It results, in other words, in something resembling the complicated and corrupt tax regime of the United States today.

If the polity wishes to promote homeownership, provide assistance to the vulnerable, encourage particular kinds of investment, foster charity, and the like, then it should do so directly—not with convoluted, inefficient, and prejudicial provisions in the tax code.

The same is true when the system privileges one kind of income over another, for then economic decision making is distorted by tax considerations. It must always be remembered that the power to tax is also the power to destroy—or, at the very least, to create perverse incentives and disincentives. Thus the propensity of governments to tax income—the fruit of people's labor and ingenuity—is wrongheaded. Taxing income discourages productivity, encourages tax avoidance (if not evasion), and engenders resentment.

A consumption tax is often proposed as an alternative, and it would indeed be far better, provided that it were not used to privilege one form of purchase over another—for instance, milk and yams over marble and yachts. Otherwise a consumption-tax regime would again be marked by political strife and corruption, as competing interests fought over rules and rates. Yet a consumption tax that did not differentiate between essentials and luxuries would be regressive, burdening the poor far more than the rich.

The ideal form of general taxation, at least in an economy with well-developed financial institutions, is therefore a transaction tax. As the name indicates, this is a small fee—say, 0.5 percent shared between payer and payee—levied on every transaction. (The rate could be adjusted annually by a fraction to keep income and outgo in balance.) This tiny fee would replace not only the income tax, but also corporate taxes, payroll taxes, excise taxes, inheritance taxes, and all the petty ways the federal government extracts revenue from persons and enterprises.[1]

Such a tax turns the economic highway into a toll road. Whenever individuals or entities bought or sold anything (even a subway token), received a credit or made a payment, or withdrew or deposited money, they would have to pay an automatic tax on that transaction—but one so small that it would not affect, much less distort, their economic behavior. Yet, in aggregate, the tax would generate vast revenues.

Because cash would pay a toll whenever it entered or exited the financial system, no one could escape the tax by operating entirely outside the formal economy. Besides, the cost to an individual of a $50,000 transaction would be a mere $125, so conspiring to evade the tax would hardly make sense, even for criminals.

Although business in general would bear most of the tax burden under such a scheme (a fact that would necessarily be reflected in consumer prices), the financial sector would be disproportionately affected, because even a minuscule tax on every one of the billions of transactions made every day would generate trillions in annual revenue, Nevertheless, the tax on any particular transaction would be so small that it should not affect business as usual—but if the tax did discourage churning in the financial casino, that might not be such a bad thing.

It may be objected that such a scheme for raising general revenue would be fair procedurally, in that the same rules would apply equally to all, but that it would not be fair socially, because it would not be progressive enough. In fact, a transaction tax would be quite progressive in one sense: it would impact primarily corporations (especially the financial sector) and, to a lesser extent, those who consume the most.

Nevertheless, even though rich individuals would pay considerably more tax than poor ones, because it is they who consume and invest the most, they would not pay *proportionately* more. Moreover, unless they were heavily involved in the financial markets, their individual tax burden would be quite small. Someone who took in and then spent $500,000 annually would pay only $2500 in direct taxes (albeit much more in indirect taxes[2]), and this paltry sum might seem trivial relative to the benefit of having a stable government that keeps the peace, enforces contracts, and in general provides for the common weal in ways that make it safe to be rich. The way to deal with this perceived inequity is with a direct tax on wealth (34. Wealth Tax).

In addition, although it is generally agreed that public health and defense are expenditures that should be borne in common, the same is not necessarily true of all public goods. For example, roads are common to all, but certain entities and individuals benefit from their use more than others. There being no such thing as a "freeway," those who receive more of the benefit should have to bear more of the burden of constructing and maintaining them (32. Use Tax).

To put it in general terms, discouraging free riders is a necessary and legitimate use of the taxing power. People should have to bear the ecological, economic, and social cost of their actions (27. Thermodynamic Economy). Similarly, there is no reason why individuals or entities should be allowed to engross common property resources, such as fish or mineral resources, as if they were free goods. Hence the necessity for severance taxes (33. Severance Tax).

To sum up, general taxation needs to be kept as simple, neutral, straightforward, economical, and effective as possible. Above all, it must be kept apolitical. Its only purpose is to collect the wherewithal for a civilized society without unduly inconveniencing the geese whose feathers are being plucked. The other forms of taxation to be considered next may make a secondary contribution to the treasury, but they should be regarded primarily as the means for achieving sustainability, equity, and justice, not raising revenue.

# 32

## Use Tax

That no one should get a free ride at public expense would seem to be self-evident (31. Tax for Revenue). However, applying this principle in practice is far from straightforward, because determining what should be borne as a common expense and what should come from the pockets of individuals or entities is inescapably a political decision. That being said, there are certain activities that are intrinsically common and that must, therefore, be funded from general revenue.

In part, the reason is practical. There is simply no way to tease out each individual's share of defense expenditures or the cost of a national communicable disease center. These and similar activities have to be paid for from the public purse.

In addition, some government programs whose benefits are less widely dispersed are almost universally regarded as a necessary and appropriate public charge. For example, although one can debate particular policies and programs, who can begrudge benefits for war veterans, especially those who have been physically or psychologically maimed while serving their country?

On the other hand, agricultural subsidies, however justifiable in principle, seem almost always to become exercises in vote buying and to have other perverse side effects. The same is unfortunately true of old-age benefits and other targeted programs. In other words, the farther away from what is undeniably common to all, the more political the decision (in the bad sense) and the greater the risk of boondoggles or outright fraud.

Yet the political is also cultural. In the United States, government support of the arts is controversial; in Germany, it is axiomatic. So Germany blooms with roughly twenty-five times the number of symphonies and opera houses per capita as in the US, a luxuriance of which the German people are justifiably proud. Thus there can be no absolute rules.

Nevertheless, it seems wise to adopt a principle that general revenue be reserved as much as possible for truly common expenditures. It follows that wherever it is practicable to separate out activities for which users can legitimately be charged, then it would be good to make people pay in proportion to the benefit received.

For instance, making highways or even city streets "free" invites overuse and precipitates the tragedy of the commons. To the extent feasible, drivers should be charged fees that accord with their usage, taking into account factors like vehicle weight and mileage. A tax on fuel might be only one component of such a tax; automatic toll collection devices embedded in cars and roadways or other technological solutions might also contribute. But however the fees are collected, the total should reflect *all* the relevant costs—that is, not just the expense of constructing, administering, and maintaining roadways *per se*, but also such related expenses as highway police, ambulances, trauma centers, and the like.

A similar logic applies to activities that inflict harm on the commons—for instance, polluting the environment. If the principle were established that no one can use, much less abuse, the commons without paying for the privilege, then the perpetrators would be strongly motivated to clean up their act, because it would be less costly than polluting.

More generally, an effective use-tax regime would foster ecological and social responsibility, because individuals would no longer be able to escape the consequences of their actions. Faced with paying the true cost of driving, individuals might find it less expensive and more agreeable to live closer to work in pedestrian- and bicycle-friendly communities served by mass transit.

In short, wherever possible, make individuals and entities bear the full cost of their acts as a way of encouraging them to be socially and environmentally responsible. That use taxes would also enrich the treasury is a welcome bonus—and one that could enable a virtuous circle, provided that the proceeds of the tax are dedicated to continuously expanding and improving infrastructure and other public facilities.

To put it the other way around, a well-designed use-tax regime would prevent the vicious circle of private affluence and public squalor that results when individuals and entities ride free on the commons.

# 33

---

## Severance Tax

Establishing an economy grounded in physical and ecological reality (27. Thermodynamic Economy) will entail a use-tax regime that makes individuals and entities pay for their use of the commons (32. Use Tax). But it will also require a regime of severance taxes that puts a price on natural resources. For when nature's bounty is treated as a free good, the tragedy of the commons is inevitable.

Take water, for example. Provided that the withdrawal rate does not exceed the recharge rate, which varies from year to year, aquifers are renewable resources. But if the price of water reflects only the cost of extraction and trans-portation—or, what is worse, if the price is subsidized—then it will be too low to prevent overuse and eventual depletion of the aquifer. The solution is a sever-ance tax that is carefully calculated and annually adjusted to keep consumption to a level that is at, or even slightly below, the recharge rate. Once consumers stop getting a free ride at the expense of nature, they will naturally conserve water or even abandon projects that no longer make economic sense at a higher price—for example, growing cotton in deserts. In consequence, demand and supply would quite naturally come into balance.

Other renewable resources can be treated in the same fashion, although the tax mechanism might be different. For instance, a severance tax on catches might replace the thicket of complex regulations that now governs fisheries. The health of the fishery would be continuously monitored and the tax adjusted accordingly—again, with the aim of keeping the exploitation rate at or slightly below the replenishment rate, so that the oceans provide a sustained yield in perpetuity.

Although getting the details of a severance tax right in the case of renewable resources would require work at the outset and continual adjustment thereafter, the criterion of success would be clear: the preservation of the resource for posterity (25. Usufruct). Thus the process would be relatively straightforward.

Nonrenewable resources present a far greater challenge. The principle is clear enough—use them not for current consumption but only for capital expenditures that benefit the future as well as the present (27. Thermodynamic Economy). However, determining the exact level of taxation that would achieve this end (so that decisions on projects did not have to be made *ad hoc*) would be daunting.

The thorny complexities are well illustrated by the case of petroleum. The current market price of petroleum is obviously far too low, because it is everywhere being used to fuel current consumption, resulting in a depletion rate that is rapidly exhausting the resource. Because petroleum in the ground is mistakenly regarded as a free good, the price reflects only the costs of extraction, transportation, and refining, plus a premium due to cartel pricing, geopolitical worries, speculative activity, and so forth. But what, then, is the true price of petroleum? That is, what is it really worth (in thermodynamic terms)?

Each barrel of petroleum can do the work of approximately thirty horses. A mature and trained draft horse with a working life expectancy of about ten years is valued at upwards of $1,000. So is each barrel worth $30,000, about three hundred times the current price? Obviously not, because the horse works day after day for ten years. On the other hand, horses eat and incur other costs that have to be factored in. However, they also reproduce themselves approximately one-and-one-half times in ten years, which adds to their value.

The calculation for petroleum is equally complex, because its use entails widespread pollution and numerous other costs, both direct and indirect (e.g., the expense of maintaining a carrier group in the Persian Gulf). Even an army of accountants would therefore struggle to establish the "true" price of petroleum. In fact, only a rough estimate seems possible. Thus it may be necessary to set the level of tax on petroleum (as well as metals, minerals, and the like) somewhat arbitrarily at first and then adjust as necessary.

With respect to energy resources, some might favor a tax on end users instead of producers. Indeed, a direct tax on energy usage is often mooted (but never passed). However, as producers are far fewer than users, it would seem to be more efficient and less costly to levy a severance tax at the mine or well-head. The cost would then be passed forward to end users, who will regulate their behavior accordingly. In general, once the principle of a severance tax is accepted, devising the mechanism for each resource would become a merely technical problem that human ingenuity can readily solve.

We now have a rough idea of what would be required to achieve the goal. Although the comparison between oil and horses has to be taken with caution—nonrenewable and renewable resources are categorically different—it does suggest that the price of almost all nonrenewable resources probably needs to be roughly an order of magnitude higher than at present to guarantee that they will be used to embellish civilization rather than to gratify desire.

# 34

## Wealth Tax

For almost all of its existence, the human race has lived in small face-to-face societies in which wealth was equally distributed. This was partly because the material conditions of life did not allow serious inequality to develop. But it was also
because virtually all primal societies institutionalized wealth redistribution in one
form or another. The skilled hunter won respect not solely because he was successful, but because he shared his bounty. And the chief obtained his prestige and
held his position precisely by virtue of his generosity, remaining chief only so long
as he gave away goods and served the tribe. The famous potlatch of the Kwakiutls
is just the most extreme example of such institutionalized redistribution.

The ancient world had something similar. Wealthy Athenians and Romans
were obliged by public pressure, if not by law, to erect temples, equip warships,
or make other contributions to the public weal. Similarly, in medieval times both
Christianity and Islam institutionalized charity, the belief that the rich have a
moral obligation to help the poor.

This historical record reflects the sense of fairness embedded in the human
psyche. It also explains why the issue of justice has preoccupied political philosophers since ancient times. The large disparities of wealth that accumulate in
industrial societies are therefore a problem simply because they violate innate
moral sentiment. Worse yet, the nature of industrial civilization greatly amplifies
the power and status conferred by the disparity in wealth. Hence to forestall a
buildup of social resentment, it is essential that those who receive disproportionate benefits also be seen to make a disproportionate contribution to the
public purse.

As noted, a tax on income is a tax on effort, ingenuity, and productivity—all traits we wish to encourage, because they benefit society even as they enrich individuals (31. Tax for Revenue). We are left, then, with no alternative but to tax wealth directly.

This bald statement may provoke outrage in some quarters, but in fact we already have such a tax—the tax on real property that is the primary support of local governments and school districts. We take it as axiomatic that those who live in hovels should pay little or nothing, while those who inhabit mansions should pay in proportion to the value of their property. This is both fair and realistic, in that those in hovels cannot really afford more. All that remains is to apply the same logic to entire estates.

In line with the general principle of taxation, the administration of such a tax should be kept as simple and as straightforward as possible. The aim should not be to squeeze so-called malefactors of great wealth for every last penny with an intrusive search for every conceivable asset but rather to impose a modest but significant tax on the most visible and easily measured aspects of an individual's worth.

In other words, it would be wise to exercise restraint. For if the rate is felt to be too high or the tax regime is experienced as predatory—or, what is worse, if it is seen to be fueled by envy rather than equity—then capital flight and other forms of tax avoidance and evasion will swiftly follow. In general, people do not mind paying a fair share, provided that the collection method is reasonable, but they bitterly resent being gouged and will respond accordingly.

To speak more generally, a wealth tax is not intended to be a major source of revenue, only to make a transaction-tax regime appear more progressive (than it already is[1]). It is therefore best understood symbolically—as a demonstration that the rich are contributing something extra to the society that enables their riches.

Taxes by themselves can never be the remedy for socioeconomic inequality. In a developed economy, nothing can prevent the natural tendency for wealth and power to accumulate at the top of the social pyramid. Yet this tendency can be moderated, and its effects made more palatable, by policies that promote greater opportunity and equity—for instance, providing a first-class education to all (22. Education for Excellence). A relatively simple and transparent wealth tax that symbolizes the willingness of the prosperous to share some of the fruits of their good fortune with the society that fostered that prosperity is an important gesture in that direction.

There will, of course, always be a few Scrooges who insist that they made their fortune entirely on their own and owe not a farthing to their fellow beings, much less to a grasping government. But given the absence of an income tax (or any other impost on individual income and assets except local property taxes), and provided that the rate and method of collection were reasonable, it seems probable that the majority of the better-off would accept a wealth tax in the spirit of *richesse oblige*.

# 35

## Graduated Prisons

No matter how excellent its mores and laws, a society is bound to have miscreants and malefactors—people who violate the society's norms and who must be dealt with accordingly. The challenge is to create a system of criminal justice that is firm yet humane, punitive but not vindictive. For a system that corrects without compassion or discrimination is not only unjust, it is also more likely to spawn rather than suppress criminality. On the other hand, a society that does not police and punish as necessary invites criminal behavior.

The solution is a graduated penal system that separates different categories of offender. Punishment would fit the crime in two ways.[1]

First, the system would differentiate between various types of crime. Instead of prisons containing mixed populations, offenders would be incarcerated separately—gang members with other gang members, sex offenders with other sex offenders, white-collar criminals with other white-collar criminals, and so forth. Even certain types of offense would need to be treated differently—for instance, the man who murders his wife in a fit of passion and the mafia assassin, the shoplifter and the career thief, and so on. If prisoners were segregated appropriately, then prisons would be less violent, simpler to manage, and better able to rehabilitate.

Second, the system would be graduated in terms of severity, separating felon from non-felon, violent from nonviolent, first-offender from recidivist, and redeemable from incorrigible. In such a system, most non-dangerous first offenders would serve their time in halfway houses or in semi-confinement—performing community service, receiving therapy, and training for a noncriminal future as they paid their debt to society. Others who were more dangerous would be truly incarcerated, yet offered ample opportunities for rehabilitation. Still others—hardened criminals, serial killers, psychopaths, and the like—would be housed in high-security penitentiaries that nevertheless offered opportunities for rehabilitation. Finally, the truly incorrigible and most dangerous would spend the rest of their days on a kind of Devil's Island.[2]

Except for the latter, prisoners would always have the possibility of promotion or relegation. Good behavior, cheerful work performance, learning an honest trade, earning a degree, genuine religious commitment, and other evidence of reform would promote a prisoner to a lesser degree of confinement and greater access to privileges.[3] The contrary would relegate a prisoner to durance more vile. Hence a prisoner's fate would be largely in his or her hands.

A prison system, however indispensable, is a last resort. Provided the society has strong mores, good laws, excellent education, and the like, the number of malefactors will be small and the prison population manageable. The antidote to crime is not punishment but a society that produces human beings instead of criminals. Indeed, if you want to know whether a society is sick or healthy, you have only to count the prisoners and see how they are treated.

# Epilogue

The preceding pattern language is not a political program to be implemented within the old framework of thought. New programs within old paradigms simply recreate the old problems in a new guise. Rather, the patterns are the practical expression of a new (yet old) philosophy of politics. Only if this philosophy is understood and accepted can the patterns serve as the basis for a politics that is sane, humane, wise, and ecological.

Nor are the patterns by themselves proof against corruption. At some point, it will seem expedient to bend the rules—for example, to run up debts and tolerate "just a little bit of inflation" rather than suffer economic pain. To adapt a famous saying of Edmund Burke, "the true danger is when [virtue] is nibbled away, for expedients, and by parts."[1] Political sanity is not easily won and easily slips away unless a people remain disciplined, resolute, and vigilant in its defense.

Even so, political entropy is, in the end, inescapable: "Experience hath shewn," said Thomas Jefferson, "that even under the best forms [of government], those entrusted with power have, in time, and by slow operations, perverted it into tyranny..."[2]

# Bibliographic Note

A bibliographic note on an immense subject with a vast literature must be either encyclopedic or brief. I will be brief.

I was inspired to do political philosophy in a different mode by Christopher Alexander et al.'s *A Pattern Language* (New York, NY: Oxford University Press, 1977). Dissatisfied with the results of an architecture based on mechanical principles, Alexander and his colleagues devised a pattern language—that is, a set of design criteria—for constructing human settlements and dwellings organically. In other words, for practicing architecture as if people mattered. I have tried to do the same for politics, to establish a pattern language of sane polity by supplying design criteria for a politics as if people mattered.

The source of almost all my ideas can be found in three previous works along with their associated references: *Ecology and the Politics of Scarcity* (San Francisco, CA: W. H. Freeman & Co., 1977); *Requiem for Modern Politics* (Boulder, CO: Westview Press, 1997); and *Plato's Revenge* (Cambridge, MA: MIT Press, 2011).

For a succinct tutorial on the lessons of history, Will and Ariel Durant's *The Lessons of History* (New York, NY: Simon and Schuster, 1968) has no equal. Drawing on a lifetime of study, the Durants' "survey of human experience" sets forth the enduring patterns that have marked all previous civilizations. Understanding these patterns provides a realistic basis for designing a polity for human beings as they actually are, instead of how we might like them to be.

Edmund Burke's *Reflections on the Revolution in France*, ed. L. G. Mitchell (New York, NY: Oxford University Press, 1999) provides an eloquent analysis of political reality. Conservative in the best sense of a word that is now mostly used as an epithet to condemn reactionaries and plutocrats, Burke argues for prudence, tolerance, and moderation as the indispensable political virtues—and for a politics grounded on the enduring reality of the human condition rather than abstract notions of right and wrong.

Along the same lines, but keyed to the American case instead of the French Revolution, Alexis de Tocqueville's *Democracy in America*, ed. Richard C. Heffner (New York, NY: Signet, 2001) addresses the challenge of reconciling democracy with liberty and other political goods. His warnings about the ways in which the fledgling democracy might go wrong were unfortunately prescient—for example, "that servitude of the regular, quiet, and gentle kind...might be combined more easily than is commonly believed with some of the outward forms of freedom [304]." Taking these warnings to heart today might provide a roadmap for returning the United States to political sanity.

In addition, we can still learn from the political wisdom of the American founders. Usually read today as a historical document rather than a guide to sane polity, *The Federalist Papers* authored by Alexander Hamilton, James Madison, and John Jay (New York, NY: Tribeca Books, 2011) contains a deep understanding of history and politics that transcends its original polemical purpose.

Finally, for a forthright and realistic view of what produces political insanity, Reinhold Niebuhr's *Moral Man and Immoral Society* (New York, NY: Charles Scribner's Sons, 1932) is still as trenchant and relevant today as it was on the day it was published.

# Notes

[1] Friedrich Nietzsche, *Beyond Good and Evil*, trans. Helen Zimmern (Radford, VA: Wilder, 2008), 56.

[2] Blaise Pascal, *Pensées*, trans. Roger Ariew (Indianapolis, IN: Hackett, 2005), 144. See also Plato, *The Laws of Plato*, trans. Thomas L. Pangle (Chicago, IL: University of Chicago Press, 1988), 192–193, where the Athenian Stranger says, "the affairs of human beings are not worthy of great seriousness; yet it is [unfortunately] necessary to be serious about them."

Preface

[1] See William Ophuls, *Ecology and the Politics of Scarcity* (San Francisco, CA: W. H. Freeman, 1977); William Ophuls, *Requiem for Modern Politics* (Boulder, CO: Westview Press, 1997); William Ophuls, *Plato's Revenge* (Cambridge, MA: MIT Press, 2011). See also William Ophuls, *Immoderate Greatness* (North Charleston, SC: CreateSpace, 2012), for the physical and political challenges that confront every form of civilization.

[2] Ophuls, *Plato's Revenge*, 104, 152–154.

[3] Ibid., 8–9, 22, 26, 42–43, 45–47.

Introduction

[1] Thomas Hobbes, *Leviathan*, ed. J. C. A. Gaskin (New York, NY: Oxford University Press, 2009), 7.

[2] Michael P. Riccards, *A Republic, If You Can Keep It* (Westport, CT: Greenwood Press, 1987), 41.

[3] William Ophuls, *Plato's Revenge* (Cambridge, MA: MIT Press, 2011), 45–60.

[4] Ibid., 109–115, 151–152. See also "Box 8.1: Planning Versus Design" in William Ophuls, *Ecology and the Politics of Scarcity* (San Francisco, CA: W. H. Freeman & Co., 1977), 228–229.

[5] Ophuls, *Plato's Revenge*, 151.

[6] James Gleick, *Chaos* (New York, NY: Viking, 1987), 110.

[7] Melvin Konner, *The Tangled Wing* (New York, NY: Holt, Rinehart and Winston, 1982), 413–414.

[8] Christopher Alexander et al., *The Timeless Way of Building* (New York, NY: Oxford University Press, 1979).

[9] Christopher Alexander et al., *A Pattern Language* (New York, NY: Oxford University Press, 1977). The first fifteen patterns deal with regional and city planning and are therefore quite political in the sense that they aspire to give a certain order and character to society.

[10] Ibid., 746–749, 876–882.

[11] Isaiah Berlin, *The Hedgehog and the Fox* (New York, NY: Simon & Schuster, 1953).

Chapter 1

[1] Wendell Berry, *The Gift of Good Land* (Berkeley, CA: Counterpoint, 2009), 281.

Chapter 3

[1] Paraphrasing Robert B. Edgerton, *Sick Societies* (New York, NY: Free Press, 1992), 70.

[2] Edmund Burke, "Letter to a Member of the National Assembly" (1791) in *Reflections on the Revolution in France*, ed. L. G. Mitchell (New York, NY: Oxford University Press, 2009), 289.

[3] Hippolyte Taine, "Notes on England," cited Gertrude Himmelfarb, *The De-moralization of Society* (New York NY: Vintage, 1996), 39.

[4] Jean-Jacques Rousseau, *On The Social Contract*, ed. Roger D. Masters, trans. Judith R. Masters (New York, NY: St. Martin's Press, 1978), 77.

Chapter 4

[1] Aristotle, *Politics*, trans. Ernest Barker (New York, NY: Oxford University Press, 1995), III, ix.

[2] Ibid., II, i.

[3] Gustave Le Bon, *The Crowd* (Mineola, NY: Dover, 2002), xiii.

[4] Walter Lippmann borrowed the Chinese concept to make this point. See Clinton Rossiter and James Lare, eds., *The Essential Lippmann* (Cambridge, MA: Harvard University Press, 1982), 208–211.

[5] Will and Ariel Durant, *The Lessons of History* (New York, NY: Simon and Schuster, 1968), 41.

[6] Ibid., 51.

[7] See fuller discussion in William Ophuls, *Plato's Revenge* (Cambridge, MA: MIT Press, 2011), 77–80, 86–87, 97–98.


Chapter 5

[1] Edmund Burke, *Reflections on the Revolution in France*, ed. L. G. Mitchell (New York, NY: Oxford University Press, 1999), 8.

[2] Niccolò Machiavelli, *The Prince*, trans. George Bull (New York, NY: Penguin, 2005), 105.


Chapter 6

[1] John Stuart Mill, *On Liberty*, ed. Gertrude Himmelfarb (New York, NY: Penguin, 1975), 63.

[2] Euripedes, *Bacchae*, trans. Paul Woodruff (Indianapolis, IN: Hackett, 1998).

[3] Clifford Geertz, "Deep Play: Notes on the Balinese Cockfight," *Daedalus* 101, No. 1 (Winter 1972): 1–37.


Chapter 7

[1] J. S. Mill, *On Liberty and Other Writings*, ed. Stefan Collini (Cambridge, England: Cambridge University Press, 1989), 114–115.

## Chapter 8

[1] Clinton Rossiter and James Lare, eds. *The Essential Lippmann* (Cambridge, MA: Harvard University Press, 1982), 19.

[2] Alexis de Tocqueville, *Democracy in America*, ed. Richard C. Heffner (New York, NY: Signet, 2001), 305.

## Chapter 9

[1] C. S, Lewis, *God in the Dock*, ed. Walter Hooper (Grand Rapids, MI: W. B. Eerdmans, 2001), 292.

## Chapter 11

[1] Letter to Mary Gladstone, April 24, 1881, in John Dalberg-Acton, *Letters of Lord Acton to Mary Gladstone*, ed. Herbert Paul (New York, NY: Macmillan, 1905), 196.

[2] Richard Hofstadter, *The American Political Tradition* (New York, NY: Vintage, 1989), 11.

## Chapter 12

[1] John Locke, *Two Treatises of Government*, 3rd. ed., ed. Peter Laslett (New York, NY: Cambridge University Press, 1988), 309, emphasis and spelling in original.

## Chapter 13

[1] Jean-Jacques Rousseau, *Émile*, trans. Allan Bloom (New York, NY: Basic Books, 1979), 473.

## Chapter 14

[1] Alexander Hamilton, James Madison, and John Jay, *The Federalist Papers* (New York, NY: Tribeca Books, 2011), 26.

[2] Jean-Jacques Rousseau, *On The Social Contract*, ed. Roger D. Masters and trans. Judith R. Masters (New York, NY: St. Martin's, 1978), 85.

[3] Ibid., 102.

[4] Speech in the House of Commons, *The Official Report, House of Commons* (5th Series), 11 November 1947, Vol. 444, 206–07.

[5] Aristotle, *The Politics*, trans. Benjamin Jowett (Mineola, NY: Dover, 2000), III, xi.

[6] Ibid., VII, iv.

[7] Letter to Samuel Kercheval, July 12, 1816, in Thomas Jefferson, *The Portable Jefferson*, ed. Merrill D. Peterson (New York, NY: Penguin, 1977), 558, emphasis in original.

[8] See also the discussion of council democracy in Hannah Arendt, *On Revolution* (New York, NY: Penguin, 2006).

## Chapter 16

[1] See, for example, Richard Scorer's "Council for Posterity" described in Richard Slaughter, *New Thinking for a New Millennium* (New York, NY: Routledge, 1996), 122–125. See also Robert A. Dahl, *After the Revolution?* (New Haven, CT: Yale University Press, 1970), 58, where Dahl asserts the necessity for competence in democracies, and William Ophuls, *Ecology and the Politics of Scarcity* (San Francisco, CA: W. H. Freeman & Co., 1977), 159–161, for a discussion of democracy versus elite rule.

[2] See Robert A. Dahl, *Democracy and Its Critics* (New Haven, CT: Yale University Press, 1991), 340. Dahl proposes a "mini populus," a group of randomly selected citizens who deliberate a particular issue for a year (with extensive support from advisors) and then pronounce a decision in the name of the people.

## Chapter 17

[1] C. G. Jung, *Memories, Dreams, Reflections*, ed. Aniela Jaffé, trans. Richard and Clara Winston (New York, NY: Vintage, 1989), 236.

[2] Alvin M. Weinberg coined the phrase. A fervent proponent of nuclear power—"electricity too cheap to meter"—he nevertheless acknowledged that society

would have to pay the price in other ways. See his "Social Institutions and Nuclear Energy," *Science* 177 (1972): 27–34.

[3] See n. 2 of Chapter 16 for Dahl's "mini populus," a jury selected at random from the general population and then intensively educated on a particular issue. This may work well for general matters—as it does in courts, where citizen-jurors for the most part exhibit competence and common sense. But technological issues require greater scientific and statistical sophistication than the majority possess. It is, for example, impossible to understand the first thing about ecology without accepting biological evolution, and poll after poll reveals that a majority of the American people either do not understand or categorically reject Darwin's great insight. And someone who barely scraped through high-school physics is ill-prepared to comprehend the pros and cons of nuclear power or the complex dynamics of the global climate regime.

[4] See n. 1 of Chapter 16.

## Chapter 18

[1] Clinton L. Rossiter, *Constitutional Dictatorship—Crisis Government in the Modern Democracies* (Princeton, NJ: Princeton University Press, 1948), remains the classic treatment of the issue.

## Chapter 20

[1] Werner Jaeger, *Paideia*, 3 vols, trans. Gilbert Highet (New York, NY: Oxford University Press, 1939, 1943, 1944), I, xxiii. See also William Ophuls, *Plato's Revenge* (Cambridge, MA: MIT Press, 2011), 97–127, for a more contemporary perspective on *paideia*.

[2] Henri Troyat, *Tolstoy*, trans. Nancy Amphoux (New York, NY: Grove Press, 2001), 152.

[3] Martin Luther King, Jr., "Facing the Challenge of a New Age," address to the Institute of Nonviolence and Social Change, Montgomery, Alabama, December 1956.

[4] C. G. Jung, *Memories, Dreams, Reflections*, ed. Aniela Jaffé, trans. Richard and Clara Winston (New York, NY: Vintage, 1989), 325.

## Chapter 21

[1] "Federalist No. 57," in Alexander Hamilton, James Madison, and John Jay, *The Federalist Papers* (North Charleston, SC: CreateSpace, 2010), 165.

[2] See William Ophuls, *Plato's Revenge* (Cambridge, MA: MIT Press, 2011), 148–150.

## Chapter 22

[1] See William Ophuls, *Plato's Revenge* (Cambridge, MA: MIT Press, 2011), 148–150. For concrete proposals see ibid., 108–125.

## Chapter 23

[1] Wendell Berry, *The Unsettling of America* (San Francisco, CA: Sierra Club, 1986), 219.

[2] Ibid.

[3] One way in which *laissez faire* might be limited is to refuse legal personality to corporations—or grant it only under much stricter conditions. If economic activity were conducted mostly by sole proprietorships and partnerships, then individuals might still become rich, but we would avoid vast accumulations of impersonal wealth and power by corporations and financiers.

[4] Edmund Burke, *Reflections on the Revolution in France*, ed. L. G. Mitchell (New York, NY: Oxford University Press, 2009), 76.

## Chapter 24

[1] John Stuart Mill, *Considerations on Representative Government* (Whitefish, MT: Kessinger Publishing, 2004), 296.

[2] See also the eighth pattern, "Mosaic of Subcultures," in Christopher Alexander et al., *A Pattern Language* (New York, NY: Oxford University Press, 1977), 42–50.

Chapter 25

[1] Letter to James Madison, September 6, 1789, in Thomas Jefferson, *The Portable Jefferson*, ed. Merrill D. Peterson (New York, NY: Penguin, 1977), 445. For Jefferson, this principle was both fundamental and "self evident."

[2] Jean-Jacques Rousseau, *On the Social Contract*, trans. Judith R. Masters, ed. Roger D. Masters (New York, NY: St, Martin's, 1978), I, viii.

Chapter 26

[1] See Chapter 17 for the full quote.

[2] Adam Smith, *The Wealth of Nations* (Hollywood, FL: Simon & Brown, 2010), 462.

[3] E. F. Schumacher, *Small Is Beautiful: Economics as if People Mattered* (Seattle, WA: Hartley and Marks, 2000).

[4] For more on frugality, see William Ophuls, *Plato's Revenge* (Cambridge, MA: MIT Press, 2011), 168, 186–187, 190–191.

[5] Conversely, strong governance is necessary to support an economy of plenitude—for example, by regulating markets and controlling the size, character, and behavior of enterprises (7. Strong Governance and 30. Market Regulation).

[6] See Ophuls, op. cit., 136–139, 143, 147, 149–150, 153–156.

[7] Letter to Samuel Kercheval, July 12, 1816, in Thomas Jefferson, *The Portable Jefferson*, ed. Merrill D. Peterson (New York, NY: Penguin, 1977), 558, emphasis in original.

Chapter 27

[1] William Ophuls, *Immoderate Greatness* (North Charleston, SC: CreateSpace, 2012), 21–29, gives a more detailed explanation of the entropy law and thermodynamic costs. See also "Box 3-5. The Thermodynamic Economy" in William

Ophuls, *Ecology and the Politics of Scarcity* (San Francisco, CA: W. H. Freeman & Co., 1977), 112-113. For more technical discussions of the thermodynamic perspective on society and economy, see Nicholas Georgescu-Roegen, "Energy and Economic Myths," *Southern Economic Journal* 41, No. 3 (January 1975): 347–381; Charles J. Ryan, "The Overdeveloped Society," *Stanford Magazine*, Fall/Winter 1979, 58–65; and Charles J. Ryan, "The Choices in the Next Energy and Social Revolution," *Technological Forecasting and Social Change* 16, No. 3 (1980): 191–208.

[2] Joseph A. Tainter, *The Collapse of Complex Societies* (New York, NY: Cambridge University Press, 1988).

[3] E. F. Schumacher, *Small Is Beautiful: Economics as if People Mattered* (Seattle, WA: Hartley and Marks, 2000), 126, 142–158, *et passim*.

[4] Ibid. See also "Box 3-6. Bulldozer Technology" and "Box 3-7. Alternative Technology" in William Ophuls, *Ecology and the Politics of Scarcity* (San Francisco, CA: W. H. Freeman & Co., 1977), 116–117, 128–129.

## Chapter 29

[1] This pattern is concerned primarily with currency inflation—that is, with the consequence of increasing the supply of currency relative to the quantity of goods. The economic pie is the same size, but there are now more dollars clamoring for slices, which effectively makes each dollar worth less. Credit expansion causes inflation in a different way—it encourages people to bid up the price of slices—but it has essentially the same effect on the society. In either case, the link between nominal price and physical reality is attenuated or even severed, with more or less traumatic results.

[2] John Maynard Keynes, *The Economic Consequences of the Peace* (New York, NY: Skyhorse Publishing, 2007 [1919]), 134.

[3] For more on the perils of inflation—even "a little bit of inflation"—see William Ophuls, *Immoderate Greatness* (North Charleston, SC: CreateSpace, 2012), 59–63, and the references thereto.

Chapter 30

[1] Karl Polanyi, *The Great Transformation*, 2nd ed. (Boston, MA: Beacon Press, 2001).

[2] Robert Kuttner, *Everything for Sale* (Chicago, IL: University of Chicago Press, 1996), 66–67.


Chapter 31

[1] See Daniel Akst, "Dreaming Out Loud: One Tiny Little Tax," *The New York Times*, February 2, 2003, which summarizes Edgar L. Feige's proposal for an automated payment transaction tax. Feige likens his idea to the E-ZPass that motorists use to pay tolls on highways. The scheme is explained in depth in Feige's "Taxation for the 21st Century: The Automated Payment Transaction (APT) Tax," presented to the President's Advisory Panel on Tax Reform, April 28, 2005. The original paper to which Akst refers was published under the same title in *Economic Policy* 15, No. 21 (October 2000), 473–511, and contains more detail than the above.

[2] Because businesses would pass the tax through to consumers, the rich would necessarily incur sizable indirect taxes just by consuming more. A transaction tax regime is, therefore, more progressive than it seems at first glance. Nevertheless, such a sophisticated argument is unlikely to persuade the average citizen that the system is progressive enough, so the rationale for a wealth tax stands (34. Wealth Tax).


Chapter 34

[1] See n. 2 of Chapter 31.


Chapter 35

[1] In what follows, I shall assume that courts observe due process, presume innocence, use untainted evidence, reject political influence, and respect the rights of defendants, so that no one is unfairly condemned. How to accomplish this is a matter of cultural preference. See Sybille Bedford, *The Faces of Justice* (New York,

NY: Simon & Schuster, 1966), which compares Anglo-American juries with the investigative magistrates used in European countries. To her surprise, Bedford was most impressed by the German system, which might, therefore, constitute a pattern for the administration of justice elsewhere.

[2] This would be a more sensible, humane, and inexpensive alternative to the costly and dehumanizing super-maximum-security prisons now used to warehouse the incorrigible. Instead of being condemned to solitary confinement in heavily guarded fortresses in perpetuity, prisoners would roam freely among their equally incorrigible fellows in isolation from the rest of humanity, part of a separate little society run largely by the prisoners themselves. This would be the most humane and cost-effective method of removing dangerous felons from society. By contrast, a criminal justice system motivated by rancor and revenge exacts a very high moral and monetary price.

[3] If there is to be a death penalty—I take no position for or against—then execution should swiftly follow sentence. Either that or allow ample opportunity for rehabilitation before finally sending a murderer to Devil's Island. To have a prisoner spend years on death row only to be executed after he or she has clearly reformed is purely vindictive and totally contrary to the ideal of compassionate justice.

Epilogue

[1] Edmund Burke, "Letter to the Sheriffs of Bristol," April 3, 1777. The original reads, "when liberty is nibbled away…"

[2] Thomas Jefferson, Preamble to "A Bill for the More General Diffusion of Knowledge," presented to the Virginia House of Delegates in 1778.

# Index